YOUR CABIN in the WOODS

by **Conrad Meinecke**

Illustrated by Victor Aures

BLACK DOG
& LEVENTHAL
PUBLISHERS
NEW YORK

Your Cabin in the Woods was originally published in 1945 and *Cabin Craft and Outdoor Living* in 1947.

Black Dog & Leventhal Publishers
Hachette Book Group
1290 Avenue of the Americas
New York, NY 10104

www.blackdogandleventhal.com

Printed in China

Cover design by Amanda Kain
and interior design by Red Herring Design.

APS

First Edition: September 2016
10 9 8 7 6 5 4 3 2 1

Black Dog & Leventhal Publishers is an imprint of Hachette Books, a division of Hachette Book Group.
The Black Dog & Leventhal Publishers name and logo are trademarks of Hachette Book Group, Inc.

The Hachette Speakers Bureau provides a wide range of authors for speaking events. To find out more, go to www.HachetteSpeakersBureau.com or call (866) 376-6591.

The publisher is not responsible for websites (or their content) that are not owned by the publisher.

Library of Congress Control Number: 2016935653

ISBN: 978-0-316-39550-2

Contents

9 Foreword
11 Lifting the Latch

13 *Your Cabin in the Woods*
18 Start Making Notes
19 Plan Wisely and You Plan for the Future
21 Who Knows? This May Be Your Future Home
23 A Cure for Restlessness

25 *One Room or Seven?*
27 The Family Camp—Summer and Winter
32 The Guest Tent for Two
35 Our Window Picture Frame

37 *Cabin Composition*
38 One-Room Cabin
40 Two-Room Cabin
    (with Storm Porch and Toilet Room)
42 Four-Room Cabin
    (with Kitchen and Storeroom)
51 The Amateur Architect

59 *Let's Go to Work*

63 **Cabin Tools—Keep 'em Sharp**
71 **Nails**
73 **Building Rules You May Not Violate**
75 **Land Cost**
76 **Cabin Cost**
77 **Logs for Your Cabin**
79 **Tie Your Cabin Together**
81 **Notching Your Logs**
83 **Cabin Detail**
85 **Windows, Doors, and Gables**
87 **Drainage and Grading**
88 **Upper and Lower Bunks Converted into Couches**
88 **Painting and Preservatives**
89 **Chinking**

91 *Indoor Fire*

93 **Fireplace Magic**
99 **Fireplaces Successfully Built by the Novice**

113 *Tricks of the Trade*

115 **Running Hot and Cold Water**
116 **Waste: Johnnies and Incinerators**

121 *Beautifying Your Cabin*
128 **Lamps, Lighting, and Illumination**
131 **Rustic Furniture**
137 **Storm Doors**
139 **Trick Door with Secret Lock**
139 **Trim Plate Decoration**
139 **Wooden-Peg Coat Hangers**
140 **Skylight**
140 **Natural Icebox Cooler**
141 **The Frame House**
144 **Flagstone Floors**
145 **Steppingstones**

147 *Personality Plus*
150 **Landscaping Your Cabin Setting**
153 **Your Flagpole**
156 **Sign Posts and Trail Markers**
157 **Let Mother Nature Be Your Gardener**
160 **Shrubs, Trees, and Reforestation**
163 **Your Treasure Chest**
169 **Sugarin'**
175 **"Tune In" on the Birds**
177 **Gateways, Guardrails, Fences, and Friendliness**
182 **Friendly Trails**
185 **Springs**

189 *Your Family Camp on Wheels*

205 *Outdoor Fires and Cooking*
209 **Make It Attractive**
212 **Outdoor Cookery in the Garden Fireplace**
236 **Picnic a la "Cart"**

237 *Great Out Doors*
242 **Security: The North Woods**
251 **Experience**
255 **Weather Wise**
260 **Night Enchantment**
261 **The Bursting Splendor of Sunrise**
262 **Woodland Sounds**
267 **When the Snow Is Deep**
272 **Friendliness**
274 **Approval**

278 **The Latchstring Is Out**
281 **About the Author**
283 **Index**

Foreword

FIRST of all, Conrad Meinecke's Cabin in the Woods is a cabin not made with hands; it is eternal in the heaven of his mind. He has roamed the Rockies, tramped the Balkans, lived in adobe, bedded down in the desert of restless sands, but always he comes back to his true love—a cabin in the woods. He has built thirty-two cabins and fireplaces in the Rockies and in Canada and now has six cabins scattered about in the Western Hemisphere.

Track of white-Tailed Deer

From his artist, linguistic father, who at ninety-three could still do a handstand, and from his Scotch-Swiss mother, who combined a practical, pioneering type of thinking with a high degree of spirituality, he inherited something in his genes that defies imprisoning in words. He is a lean, tough specimen illuminated by a quenchless inner fire of spirituality. His tireless energy, his buoyancy, and, strange to say, his quietness of spirit, spring from his communion with forms, visible and invisible, of the Great Out Doors. At some time, like his grand old father, he has had a draught from the fabled fountain of Immortal Youth. He is fortunate in his ancestry—the genes somehow "blended" just right.

Fore and hind foot Tracks of Red Fox

Curiously enough, with this idealism, this high spirituality, this understanding love of the inner meaning of life, he combines a Yankee, practical ingenuity. He is the best cook that ever concocted a meal for me in the wilderness. He "swings a mean skillet." If he says, "Build your fireplace so and so," do it. And when you have

9

Fore and hind foot tracks of Skunk

Cottontail Tracks

done it, you can stretch your moccasined feet to the fire and have no smoke in your eyes. Build your cabin the way he tells you and you will have a joy forever, partly because you built it and partly because it "belongs" to the particular spot of its own earth, partly because it's as handy as a pocket in a shirt, and then, too, because it's easy on your income.

This man tramps all over the earth and, when he settles down, builds himself a "nest" on the end of a twig as practical and as intriguing as that of the Baltimore oriole. Somehow, he has so much—maybe it is because he is always giving it away.

From being a successful young man in business affairs, he turned to working with and for men and boys. Somehow, he has in his spiritual heritage and in his ripening wisdom, the blessedness of sharing. From his Cabin in the Woods, you can learn how to fashion *your* cabin, but more, you may become more fit to live in a "house not made with hands, eternal in the heavens."

Elbert K. Fretwell
Chief Scout Executive (1943–1948)
Boy Scouts of America

Lifting the Latch

Fore and hind foot tracks of Raccoon

THERE is nothing unusual in these pages. There is little I may claim as original. Some of the material here treated is as old as time. Many friends and books have contributed to its contents. My thirty years of outdoor experience and cabin building may, however, save the reader much of the trial-and-error method when he builds his Cabin in the Woods.

I have attempted, most of all, to help build an attitude of mind toward the Great Out Doors— an appreciation of simple living. I want to influence both men and women toward the belief and confidence they are "masters of their destiny" if they can stay within the realm of their own potentialities; if they can find a normal "out" for their abilities in this creative field of the outdoors. Indeed, they can be "master builders" in the best sense. Resourcefulness, initiative, and a love for things natural—these are the values that may give us a new concept of simple living in a very complicated and mechanical civilization.

You, too, can build a Cabin in the Woods. Cabin building is fun and satisfying, and here you can learn to be a master builder instead of just a helper. Detailed and minute descriptions of every step in building a cabin can prove confusing and discouraging to the novice. If you wish to study beyond the information here given, you will find ample help in your public library. You will naturally go through that period of experimentation that is the trial-and-error method. Your trials, however, need not be crowded with too many errors.

Squirrel Tracks

11

Fore and hind
foot tracks of
Skunk

Cottontail
Tracks

I am counting on that great American quality, "horse sense." So go to it, Mr. Cabin-Builder. Keep in mind you are going to build a better and bigger cabin someday. In your first experiment, fortified by all the descriptive material you can understand and assimilate, wade in and go to work. Do it courageously and don't you dare apologize for mistakes made. You won't make the same mistake twice. Besides building your first cabin, you will absorb techniques so essential—a combination of theory and practice.

In fireplace building, the feel of a trowel in your hand; the skill of "slinging the mud" to recognize cement, sand and water mixed to the right consistency, and what it means to "sweeten" or "temper" the mixture—all these will find their rightful places and give you skills. They do not come from books alone.

Again, the art of pulling a crosscut saw; the swinging of the axe and the making of the chips to fly; the choice of axe handle that fits your grip and your height—these skills we develop through the doing.

This book is written for those who would "revert back to the land"—land near your city home—five, ten, or thirty miles—a place that can be used weekends and on vacations; indeed, throughout the year. It is written, too, for the "poor" man, that is, the man not rich in worldly goods, but rich in dreams, imagination, resourcefulness, and a willingness to make it happen.

Bless those folks who can wrest from the earth its richness, its wealth, its natural resources, and find its peace. That is our God-given right.

Your Cabin
in the
Woods

SO you are another lover of the out of doors who desires a cabin or shelter in the woods! I salute you. I understand you. I know your kind. You carry the spirit of our ancestors. The spirit of the "Great Out Doors." The first letters of these three words spell GOD. There is an irresistible force in the Great Out Doors—the very soul of America. This is as it should be.

And so from the start, let me chat with you in a very personal way. Let's take each other at face value. I picture you as sitting on a log, dressed in colorful outdoor togs while I am nestled against the notch in a big tree, hugging my knees—eager to talk it over. I feel somehow that we both want this cabin to represent our own handicraft. It must be cozy, equipped with comforts—beds, cots, or bunks according to our own fancy. It must be made bright and warm with a glowing fireplace. It must have rustic furniture and, at least, a five-foot bookshelf of our own choice of books. Old-fashioned kerosene lamps again become a luxury as they throw their soft flickering shadows.

The howling wind, the sleet driving with an impact against our tightly built cabin will only add to the security and snugness inside. Add another log to the fire. Readjust the cushions and let the world go by. This is life—with a friend who understands. Snugness and security in our Cabin in the Woods, be it sunshine or tempest. This is life.

Because we are used to city houses with a multiplicity of household duties, our Cabin in the Woods should be built where there is quiet; where housework can be reduced to a minimum; where our time may be given over to the perusal of a few chosen books; where reflection may have its full sway; where one may be carefree in the Great Out Doors. Here, for a brief spell, we may find in its very fullness, "life, liberty and the pursuit of happiness."

So now, "partner on the log" opposite, let us plan our Cabin in the Woods. Which shall it be—a log cabin or a frame building? There really is not much difference in the planning.

First, let us not be too concerned about the whole venture. The cost of land need not be prohibitive. The problem of the distance from town can be solved. Building costs, how to get logs, transportation, reforestation, trails and trail markers, gateways and fences, sanitation, lighting, lamps, and many other questions will be discussed. If the desire is there and the will to see it through, the building of Your Cabin in the Woods will be fun. Resourcefulness and initiative will meet the challenge. Most important of all, let us take our time. Let us plan carefully. Let us get as much enjoyment in the building as in the finished cabin.

A cabin and campsite in the woods, after all, should never be finished, for when there is nothing new to develop or nothing to be added, there will be little fun.

Start Making Notes

IN the original privately printed edition of this book, ample margins and blank pages afforded room for personal notes, plans, sketches, photos, and clippings; also for signatures of friends who helped plan or build the Cabin in the Woods.

In this edition, most of the blank pages are omitted, but the margins are generous, and you will find other open spots at the beginning and end of some chapters. Use them, from the start, to collect material for your cabin-building program. They will not only prove invaluable later, but will make this book truly yours, expressing your own individuality, and honoring the author by permitting him to collaborate with you in producing your own exclusive volume— *your* Cabin in the Woods.

Plan Wisely and You Plan for the Future

ABOVE all things, let us not plan too quickly, build hurriedly, or lay out our grounds haphazardly. Let us not be concerned if we do not accomplish this in a week, or a month, or even in a year. I knew a man who built a shack in the woods. It was little better than a woodshed. The next year he needed another room so he tacked a lean-to on one side. Then he added another and another. The roof looked like an ocean of waves. When he finished, his place looked like a big sprawling shack. No general floor level—no plan; low ceilings, poor ventilation. What a mess. He did not plan wisely. He is the kind of fellow who says, "If I were to do it again, I'd do so and so."

So, Mr. Cabin-Builder, I say plan wisely. Spend a summer on your site in a tent before you build. Study the air currents that flow down the hills; the prevailing winds; the landscape and vista you want to develop. Do you prefer sunrise to sunset? If you do not enjoy sunrise, then set your cabin so the morning sun will not disturb your sleep. You may enjoy the sunset from your porch or big window. Where are the noises from highways and how can you plant trees to blot out ugly views or even some of the noise?

Lastly, blueprint your newly acquired playground. Pace it off at two-hundred-foot intervals, both ways. Do this if you have an acre or one hundred acres. Record in your field notes what you find—springs, gullies, kinds of trees, bushes, rocks, ground erosion, and, if you find the latter, seek advice on what to plant to overcome this hazard.

You will discover more natural resources and materials, which you can use later and you will know where to find them when you need them. On your master blueprint, locate your yearly tree plantings, roadways, trails, springs, dates of events, et cetera. It will prove a storybook of Your Cabin in the Woods.

Who Knows?

This May Be Your Future Home

MAY I now invite you to deeper thought in your planning? Who knows what ten years from now will hold for you. You may consider retirement and make your future home in this spot of your dreams. Then again, you may turn farmer on a small scale—chickens, perhaps a pig, a cow, and a garden spot. Start a beehive or two— honey is stored in the flowers about your place. Don't close your mind to the thought. You may discover your greatest contentment and happiness, also skills and aptitudes you did not know you had. That's what our pioneer fathers did. It was about their only choice in those days.

This idea may provide a means of escape from the reality and tension of city life. It may prove a step forward and upward in the fulfillment of your life's ambitions.

Life, after all, need not be measured in accomplishment of wealth, great achievement, nor by standards of public opinion. If you have a partner who thinks likewise and is not regimented by conventional thinking, then I say, Mr. Cabin-Builder, lay your plans boldly—whether you go to the wilds of Africa, to the South Sea Islands, or to Your Cabin in the Woods—so long as you go you may find life, liberty, and ultimate happiness.

A Cure for Restlessness

YOUR Cabin in the Woods can be a perfect cure for restlessness. If you are restless today, you may be even more restless ten years from now—unless you do something about it now. Life brings increasing cares. So going to your dream spot month after month, year in and year out, you will experience a recharging, a rehabilitation, a re-creating.

Your Cabin in the Woods should always present enough challenge to keep you constantly adding to its loveliness. In this way, after each visit, you will return to your city life rested, stronger, revived.

It is obvious, then, we should take our time—months, years, predicating our building on long-term planning.

Take full enjoyment in the building. Take time to rest. Most city folks seem always to rush things through. Why? Lay off until tomorrow. Take an afternoon nap. Stop the clock for the weekend. Get off to an early start in the cool of tomorrow morning. You may be crowded in your work in town, but this should be your rest-cure, your re-creating. Don't spoil it by city-driving standards. Set your own pattern. You will be rewarded with increasing peace of mind from year to year.

Again, I say, here is a perfect cure for restlessness.

One Room
or Seven?

AND now for a word about the size of the cabin itself. Have you, in the back of your head, some notion of a three-, five-, or seven-room building? You have a big family? You need guest rooms?

The Family Camp—
Summer and Winter

I HAVE in my own cabin-site accommodations for fourteen people. But they are
not all in one building. I, too, had many
to provide for, but I started simply some twenty
years ago with a plan.

First, we built a large living room, eighteen
by twenty-four feet—with a good foundation,
large windows; in fact one window with forty-
nine panes in it measured eight feet wide by six
and one-half feet high and afforded a five-mile
view across the valley.

We included a big fireplace. Later we added
a spacious porch on two sides. On a third side,
we added a kitchen and a combination wash and
dressing room. No bath. The shower was placed
under the porch. The north end of the porch
supplied what we called the "master bedroom"—
twin beds. The porch today is enclosed richly
with woodbine.

As our needs grew, we added nine-by-twelve-
foot tents—two beds in each, a locker, chairs,
et cetera. Finally, there were four tents added
and we were set for the summers. With this

arrangement, there was freedom for everyone—more independence and plenty of privacy. One member of the party could retire or take an afternoon nap while the rest of the group would be free to play without concern about those who wanted quiet.

This, of course, did not take care of our winter needs. But, as one of the tents had served its time, we replaced it with a lovely one-room bedroom cabin with a large porch. It was finished with pine board and included a clothes closet, washstand, and a large fireplace. This bedroom cabin, which is our latest addition not more than two hundred feet away from our main living room cabin, is nestled on the hillside and is the envy of everyone who sees it. In summer, we sleep on the screened-in porch.

Thus, we have built a seven-room house—each room with an outlook on four sides, plenty of ventilation, privacy—all with real comfort.

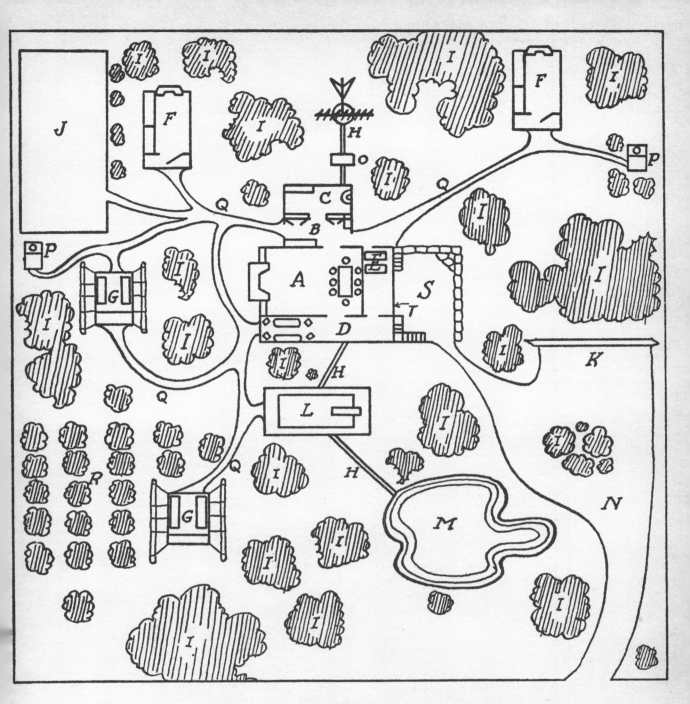

LEGEND OF FAMILY CAMP GROUNDS

A. Main Living Room
B. Kitchen
C. Wash and Storeroom
D. Veranda
E. "Master Bedroom" on Porch
F. Guest Cabin
G. Guest Tent
H. Windmill and Water System
I. Shade Trees
J. Tennis Court or Vegetable Plot
K. Parking Lot

L. Swimming Pool, 9 by 15 feet
M. Lily Pond
N. Driveway
O. Hot Water Heater
P. "Johnnie"
Q. Trails
R. Fruit Trees
S. Sunken Garden—Outdoor Fireplace
T. Shower Under Veranda

THE FAMILY CABIN AND FLOOR PLAN

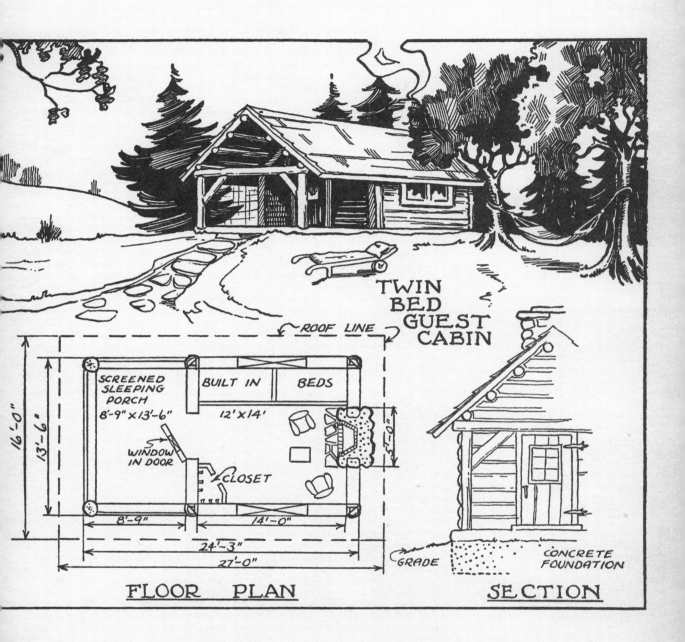

TWIN BED GUEST CABIN

FLOOR PLAN

SCREENED SLEEPING PORCH 8'-9" x 13'-6"

BUILT IN BEDS 12' x 14'

WINDOW IN DOOR

CLOSET

ROOF LINE

16'-0"

13'-6"

5'-0"

8'-9"

14'-0"

24'-3"

27'-0"

SECTION

GRADE

CONCRETE FOUNDATION

THE·FAMILY·CAMP·GUEST·TENT

TENT
FLY

The Guest Tent for Two

A TENT, fly, tent frame, and platform can be had inexpensively. With care, your bedroom tent with a fly will last about eight to ten years. The fly will give you a guarantee against leaking. Also, when anchored to side posts it will keep your tent fixed and secure against storms. The platform will give you a level floor and add dryness and cleanliness.

Eight-ounce duck canvas, double filled, is heavy enough for this size tent. Hang the tent over a wood frame and fasten all around the

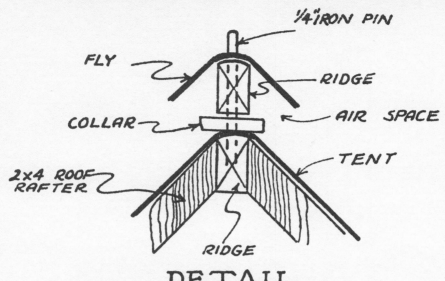

¼" IRON PIN

FLY

RIDGE

COLLAR

AIR SPACE

TENT

2x4 ROOF RAFTER

RIDGE

DETAIL

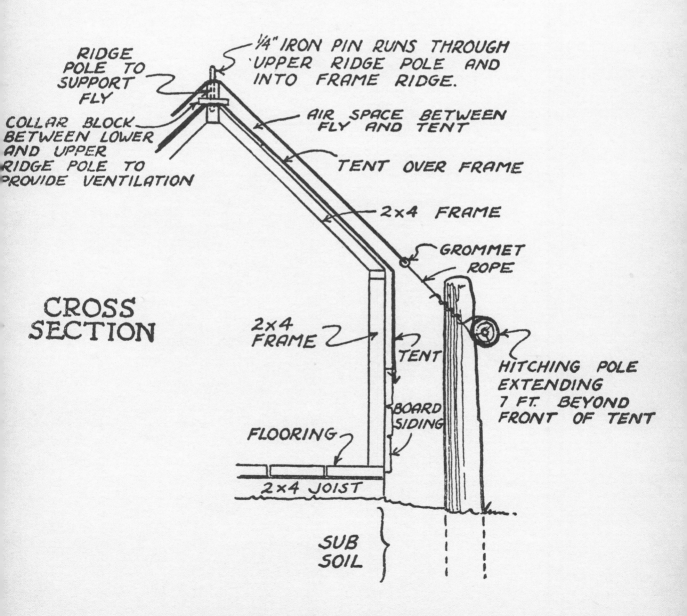

RIDGE POLE TO SUPPORT FLY

COLLAR BLOCK BETWEEN LOWER AND UPPER RIDGE POLE TO PROVIDE VENTILATION

¼" IRON PIN RUNS THROUGH UPPER RIDGE POLE AND INTO FRAME RIDGE.

AIR SPACE BETWEEN FLY AND TENT

TENT OVER FRAME

2x4 FRAME

GROMMET ROPE

CROSS SECTION

2x4 FRAME

TENT

HITCHING POLE EXTENDING 7 FT. BEYOND FRONT OF TENT

BOARD SIDING

FLOORING

2x4 JOIST

SUB SOIL

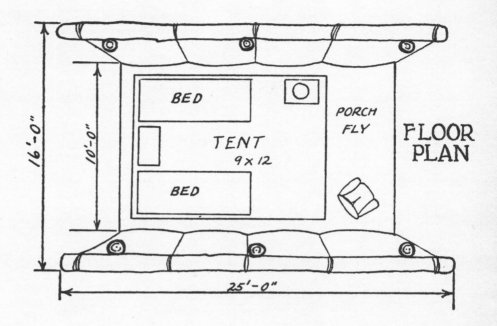

FLOOR
PLAN

16'-0"

10'-0"

25'-0"

BED

BED

TENT
9 x 12

PORCH
FLY

bottom. Guy ropes are not needed. The tent wall is two feet and six inches high. Therefore, to have standing room, a frame wall is built to be four feet and six inches with two-foot board siding below.

A nine-by-twelve-foot tent is large enough for twin beds, a dresser, washstand, and rug.

Tent fly, if ten feet by sixteen feet with air space between fly and tent, will help keep your tent cool in hot weather and provide a four-foot porch. On warm sunny days, roll up the canvas walls, let the breezes through, and make the hillside part of your living quarters.

Our Window Picture Frame

T HE big window in our cabin resembles a
picture frame in which miles of landscape
across the valley bring nature's choicest
pictures to life. Each hour of the day brings
intriguing new vistas, changing lights and shadows.

The early morning sun lights up the sparkling lily pond below us, which, in turn, throws playful, mischievous lights about us. As the day wears on, pastoral scenes replace the picture of the misty morning and through our "picture frame" we see the hillside dotted with lowing cattle, green fields boxed in with rail fences, and lined with small trees and bushes—telling the story of the toil and accomplishment of our neighboring farmers. An occasional tall elm or maple stands as a sentinel in the march of time. Far beyond "stately ships of fleecy white clouds sail majestically across the dark blue ocean of the sky," leaving one in awe, for such scenery is painted only with bold strokes by the hand of the Master Painter.

Even the sundial on a cloudy day seems to reflect our mood of response to nature—and so time passes on. Finally, lengthening shadows, dissolving glory of eventide—night—twinkling stars and a full moon.

Whenever you look out of a window, whatever the view, try to remember you are looking at one of God's great pictures.

There never were paintings comparable to those in the big window of our Cabin in the Woods.

Cabin
Composition

One-Room Cabin

HERE is the perfect, yet simplest, two-person log cabin you can wish for, low in cost and easy to build. It can be constructed as small as nine by twelve feet (inside measurement), or twelve by fourteen, fourteen by eighteen, or even larger. The larger cabin needs added structural material.

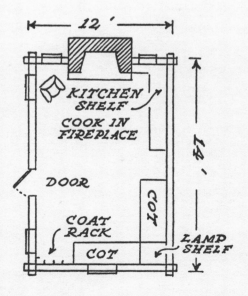

Let's discuss the nine-by-twelve-foot two-person log cabin—just one room with two commodious couches, each with a view of the fireplace. A kitchenette, quite complete. Next to the fireplace, two comfortable chairs, and a table. It's the very essence of snugness. It can be ventilated easily at upper gables without creating a draft. A floor of flagstones.

If you have natural material on your cabin site such as logs and stones, you will only have to purchase such material as cement, boards to cover your roof, shingles, windows, nails, a bit of lumber for the inside.

VIEW FROM FIREPLACE

Two-Room Cabin
(with Storm Porch and Toilet Room)

THIS cabin has the added storm porch and toilet room. The cabin proper is the same. The added storm porch offers a bit more comfort and refinement without adding much to the cost. The toilet—a slop bucket with seat and cover and pipe vent running to the outside make this type free from odors. The bucket is emptied from time to time in the backyard toilet. It serves its best purpose for winter use, when one does not gather much enthusiasm, especially on a stormy night, to visit the backyard "Johnnie." An oil heater will keep this room comfortable. Then there is the washstand. Improvise your own supply water tank; also drain the stationary with pipe to the outside. Note, also, the neatly piled wood within the storm porch. Nothing like having dry wood to start your fire, especially if you arrive on a

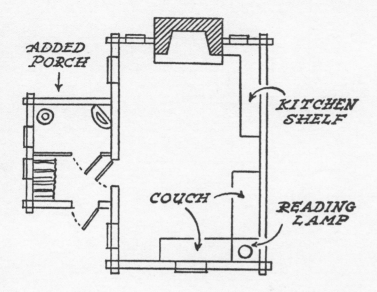

stormy night. A nine-by-twelve-foot cabin can be comfortably heated by the fireplace.

You can have an inexpensive cabin if you supply your own labor—that is, do it yourself, and if much of the natural material is on the land for the taking. A nine-by-twelve log cabin will require fourteen logs (seven inches in average thickness) twenty-one feet long; also sixteen poles (four and a half inches in average thickness) eight feet long for the roof rafters.

Enlarged Detail of Added Porch

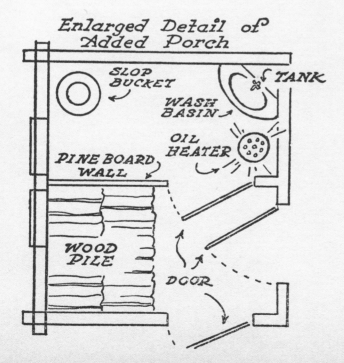

Four-Room Cabin
(with Kitchen and Storeroom)

NOW we come to the spreading idea. Obviously, it would not be satisfactory, if you have more than two to provide for, to build on the front and back the added rooms here suggested on a nine-by-twelve cabin. You may now want to build your prize cabin with living room, say fourteen by eighteen or larger. However, the nine by twelve can still enjoy a lean-to on the back by cutting a door as indicated in this floor plan. The kitchen would be small—about six by six feet, but, if carefully planned, with a small stove, shelves, etc., it will enrich even a small cabin.

You will never have greater enjoyment out of any cabin in the woods than the nine-by-twelve log cabin for two. It's snug. It suggests teamwork. It invites consideration. It is rudely complete. It provides the perfect setting for ideal companionship.

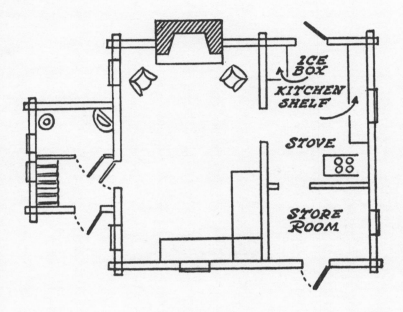

ICE
BOX

KITCHEN
SHELF

STOVE

STORE
ROOM

VIEW FROM COUCH

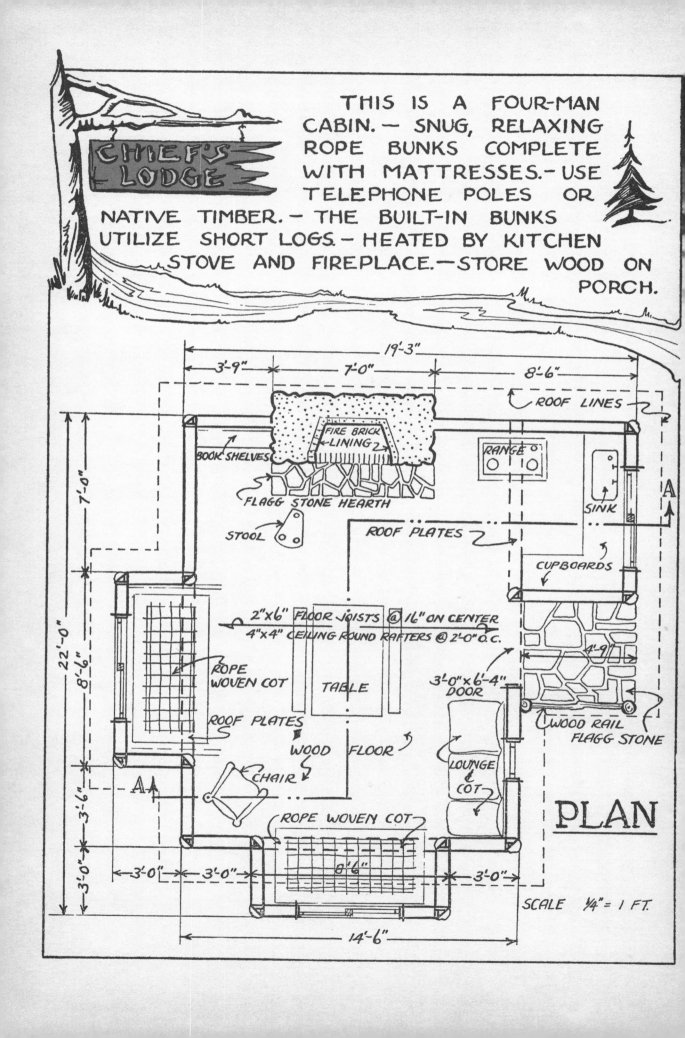

THIS IS A FOUR-MAN CABIN. — SNUG, RELAXING ROPE BUNKS COMPLETE WITH MATTRESSES. — USE TELEPHONE POLES OR NATIVE TIMBER. — THE BUILT-IN BUNKS UTILIZE SHORT LOGS. — HEATED BY KITCHEN STOVE AND FIREPLACE. — STORE WOOD ON PORCH.

CHIEF'S LODGE

PLAN

SCALE ¼" = 1 FT.

TOP OF RIDGE

SHINGLES
SHEATHING
2"x6" RAFTERS

2"x4"
BRACES

5'-4"

VENT TO EXTEND
ABOVE PEAK OF ROOF

TOP OF
PLATE

6'-8"

WOOD
STORAGE

FLOOR LINE

2"x6" JOISTS

STONE FOUNDATIONS OR CONCRETE

BELOW FROST

GRADED

SECTION TAKEN ON LINE "AA"

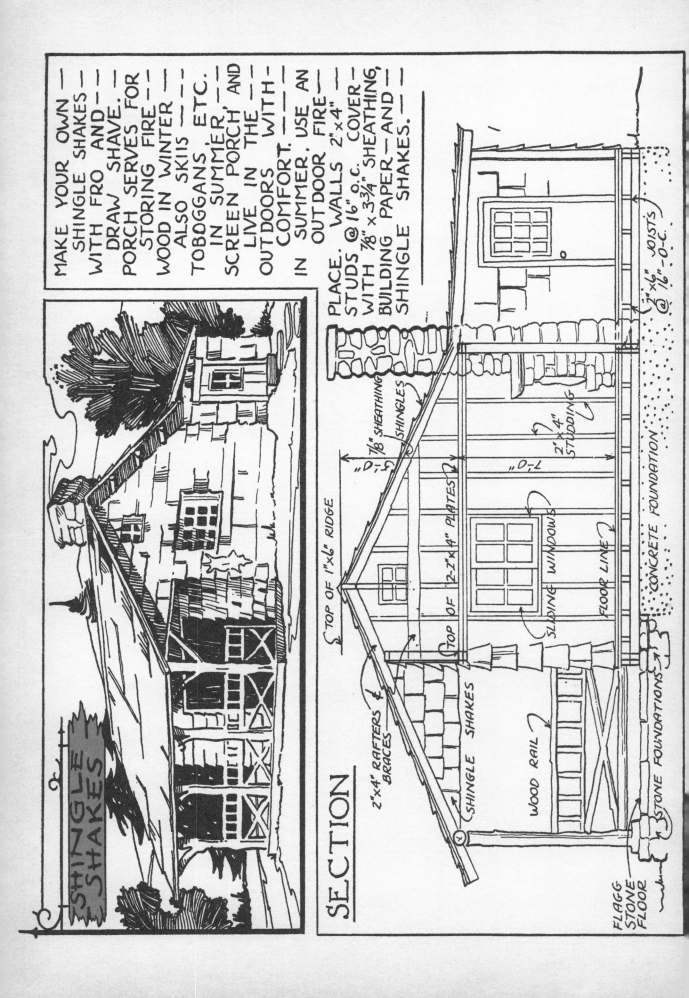

MAKE YOUR OWN — SHINGLE SHAKES — WITH FRO AND — DRAW SHAVE. — PORCH SERVES FOR — STORING FIRE — WOOD IN WINTER — ALSO SKIIS — TOBOGGANS ETC. — IN SUMMER — SCREEN PORCH AND — LIVE IN THE — OUTDOORS WITH — COMFORT. — IN SUMMER, USE AN — OUTDOOR FIRE — PLACE. WALLS 2"x4" — STUDS @ 16" o.c. COVER — WITH 7/8" x 3-3/4" SHEATHING, — BUILDING PAPER — AND — SHINGLE SHAKES.

SHINGLE SHAKES

SECTION

TOP OF 1"x6" RIDGE

2"x4" RAFTERS & BRACES

SHINGLE SHAKES

TOP OF '2-2"x4" PLATES'

7/8" SHEATHING

SHINGLES

2"-0"

7'-0"

2"x4" STUDDING

SLIDING WINDOWS

FLOOR LINE

WOOD RAIL

CONCRETE FOUNDATION

2"x6" JOISTS @ 16"-0-C.

STONE FOUNDATIONS

FLAGG STONE FLOOR

FLOOR PLAN OF "SHINGLE SHAKES"

FOR SIMPLER LIVING AND CONSTRUCTION, KITCHEN AND TOILET MAY BE LEFT OFF. COOK IN FIREPLACE.

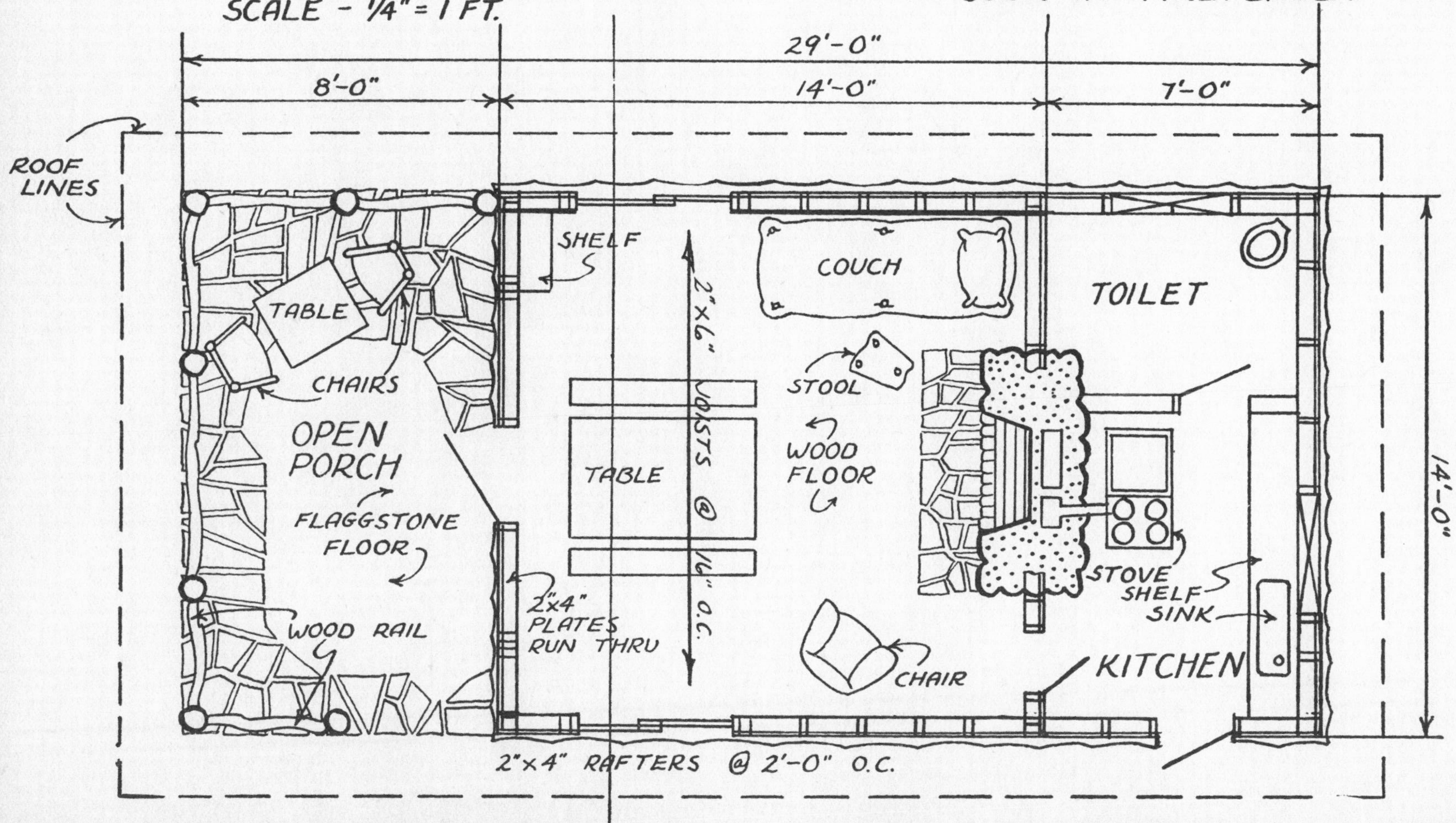

SCALE – ¼" = 1 FT.

14'-0"

7'-0"

14'-0"

29'-0"

8'-0"

TOILET

KITCHEN

STOVE
SHELF
SINK

CHAIR

COUCH

STOOL

WOOD FLOOR

2"×6" JOISTS @ 16" O.C.

TABLE

SHELF

2"×4" PLATES RUN THRU

2"×4" RAFTERS @ 2'-0" O.C.

OPEN PORCH

FLAGGSTONE FLOOR

TABLE

CHAIRS

WOOD RAIL

ROOF LINES

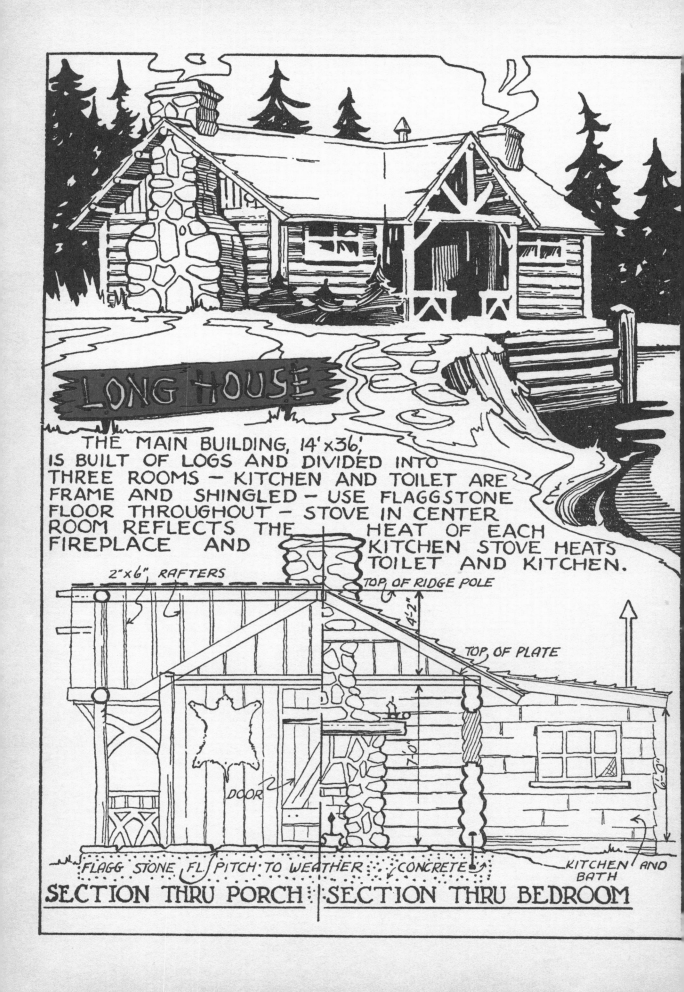

LONG HOUSE

THE MAIN BUILDING, 14'x36', IS BUILT OF LOGS AND DIVIDED INTO THREE ROOMS — KITCHEN AND TOILET ARE FRAME AND SHINGLED — USE FLAGGSTONE FLOOR THROUGHOUT — STOVE IN CENTER ROOM REFLECTS THE HEAT OF EACH FIREPLACE AND KITCHEN STOVE HEATS TOILET AND KITCHEN.

2"x 6" RAFTERS

TOP OF RIDGE POLE

4'-2"

TOP, OF PLATE

7'-0"

7'-0"

DOOR

FLAGG STONE FL. PITCH TO WEATHER   CONCRETE

KITCHEN AND BATH

SECTION THRU PORCH | SECTION THRU BEDROOM

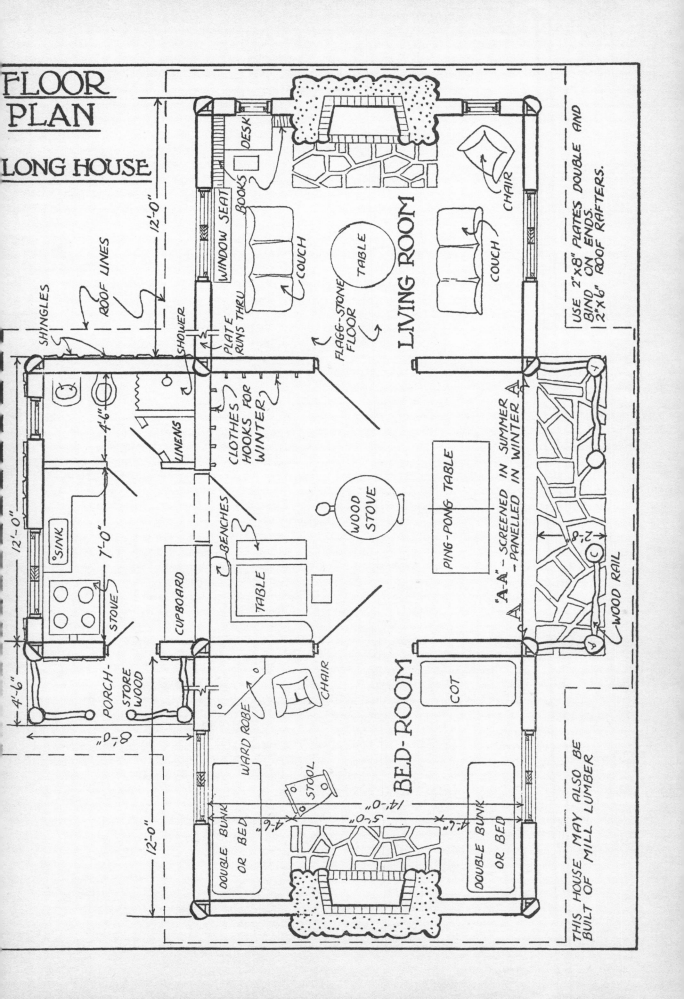

FLOOR PLAN

LONG HOUSE

LIVING ROOM

BED-ROOM

DESK

WINDOW SEAT

BOOKS

COUCH

TABLE

CHAIR

COUCH

SHINGLES

ROOF LINES

SHOWER

PLATE RUNS THRU

FLAGG-STONE FLOOR

LINENS

CLOTHES HOOKS FOR WINTER

WOOD STOVE

SINK

BENCHES

TABLE

CUPBOARD

PING-PONG TABLE

WOOD RAIL

PORCH-STORE WOOD

STOVE

WARD ROBE

CHAIR

STOOL

DOUBLE BUNK OR BED

COT

DOUBLE BUNK OR BED

"A-A"- SCREENED IN SUMMER - PANELLED IN WINTER

12'-0"

4'-6"

7'-0"

12'-0"

4'-6"

8'-0"

12'-0"

14'-0"

5'-0"

4'-6"

7'-6"

2'-6"

USE 2"x8" PLATES DOUBLE AND BIND ON ENDS. 2"x6" ROOF RAFTERS.

THIS HOUSE MAY ALSO BE BUILT OF MILL LUMBER.

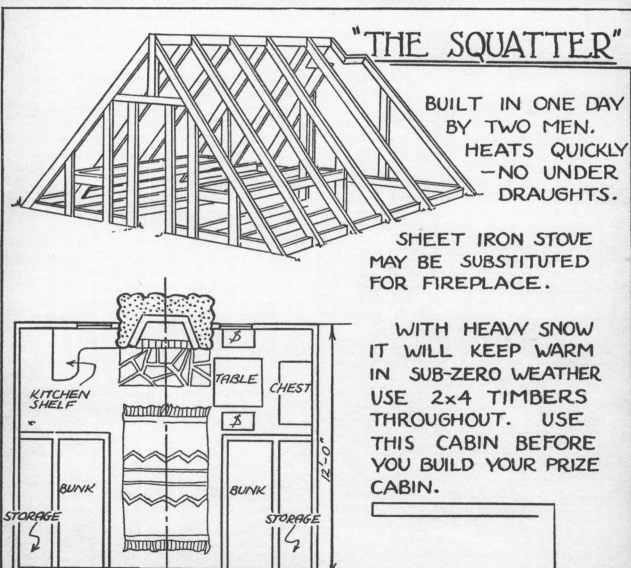

"THE SQUATTER"

BUILT IN ONE DAY BY TWO MEN. HEATS QUICKLY —NO UNDER DRAUGHTS.

SHEET IRON STOVE MAY BE SUBSTITUTED FOR FIREPLACE.

WITH HEAVY SNOW IT WILL KEEP WARM IN SUB-ZERO WEATHER USE 2x4 TIMBERS THROUGHOUT. USE THIS CABIN BEFORE YOU BUILD YOUR PRIZE CABIN.

KITCHEN SHELF

TABLE

CHEST

BUNK

BUNK

STORAGE

STORAGE

12'-0"

The Amateur Architect

WHEN planning a home of several rooms in which the cellar, first floor, second floor, attic, also bath, are involved, one does not save money by being his own architect. But to plan your own Cabin in the Woods, of one or two or three rooms, by all means be your own amateur architect. Even though you have had no experience, here are some very simple rules and methods to help you. Above all, you will get a real thrill in doing your own planning.

Cabin planning is different from planning a city home. First, there is little need for a cellar, so start with a good foundation. So many would-be cabin builders think they can save money by building a cabin on concrete piers—one at each corner of the cabin. This is getting off to a very bad start. Piers settle until, finally, the cabin floor is no longer level—cracks appear in the walls and the cabin is no longer snug and tight. A good eight-inch concrete wall all around will prove cheapest in the end. It must go below the frost line, i.e., three and a half feet below ground level in New York State. A twelve-inch footing for the eight-inch wall is desirable.

Let's take, for example, a cabin with a combination living room and dining room, porch, kitchen, and bath. Size overall, 18 feet by 32 feet. After the concrete is poured, bury one-half- or five-eighths-inch bolts in the soft cement. The bolts should be long enough to sink eight inches into the cement and protrude upward to bolt down the first log. (In frame building, enough to bolt through two two-by-four sills.)

But now let's get back to the floor plan. In these pages, you will find many suggestions of cabins, bay windows, rustic doors and windows, built-in features for books, cupboards, nooks, window seats, etc. I have avoided detailed floor plans, for after all, it should be your cabin, not mine. Your conception of room sizes will naturally differ from mine. I do, however, present some methods. Talking toward some simple principles will prove more helpful than trying to tell my reader how to proceed at every step.

Let us then look at the overall picture, from size of cabin to cupboards, furniture—yes, rugs—to fit the plan. How much furniture will be included: beds, tables, cupboards, etc.? How much space will the fireplace take? Doors should be two feet, eight inches wide, by at least six feet, six inches high. Windows to fit in between, and sized to suit one's fancy. Most log cabins are spoiled with small windows. A modern log cabin must have large windows to provide plenty of light. In one of my cabins, which measures fourteen feet by sixteen feet, I have an end window measuring six feet by eight feet, which not only gives a burst of light within, but also provides a beautiful view over the countryside.

CONSIDER EACH SQUARE AS ONE FOOT

BRACES

RAFTERS

SHINGLES

SHINGLE
SHAKES

WOOD RAIL

SLIDING
WINDOWS

STUDDING

FLOOR LINE

FLAGSTONE FLOOR

STONE
FOUNDATIONS

CONCRETE
FOUNDATION

JOISTS

ROOF LINES

SHELF

COUCH

TOILET

TABLE

CHAIRS

STOOL

SHELF

OPEN
PORCH

TABLE

FLAGSTONE
FLOOR

STOVE

SINK

CHAIR

KITCHEN

WOOD RAIL

The accompanying map of quadrille paper will help lay out the first floor plan in the minutest detail. Consider each square equal to one foot. It is obvious, then, if the cabin is to be thirty-two feet long and eighteen feet wide, we need to count the exact number of squares to get a fair picture of the size of the cabin. Just where shall we place the bed and how much space will it take? At this point, take a yardstick and measure the bed. Three feet wide by six feet, six inches long? Again we count off the same number of squares and will be amazed to find how much space it really takes in relation to the room itself. If two comfortable lounging chairs are to be included, then measure these, too, and draw them in the floor plan. A fireplace requires about seven feet by three feet of floor space, if you want an open hearth three feet wide. Cupboards, table, and other furniture must also be included.

At this point, we may find we need a larger cabin to house all the comforts desired. Remember, the man who says after his cabin is finished, "If I were to build again, I'd do so and so . . . " So, Mr. Amateur Architect, you will do well to spend winter evenings in laying out your floor plan on paper. After the floor plan, use the quadrille paper again to plan the sidewalls, again one square to the foot. Raise or lower the roof to give your cabin graceful lines. Draw in the doors and windows to scale. A log cabin in which the gable is included as part of the main living room leaves one free to start with lower sidewalls, i.e., a seven-foot sidewall is ample with the roof slanting upward to a thirteen-, fourteen-, or fifteen-foot peak, according to one's fancy. When laying out the floor plan, make all measurements starting from the inside of the cabin. Then add the thickness of the walls on the outside. Another common error made in cabin construction is to be skimpy about the overhanging roof. The cabin here described can well afford to have an overhang of eighteen inches to two feet, especially on the gable ends.

MODEL BUILDING

After your cabin plans are complete, build a miniature cabin. If you are unfamiliar with reading blueprints, the miniature cabin will prove most helpful. More than this, it will serve as a perfect guide, and save errors and expense.

Every person who has ever built a house of any kind says without fail, "If I were to build again . . ." No great project was ever built before a model was built, to visualize to the unskilled mind just what it would look like. So with us, the building field is new and we need to proceed carefully. More than this, with a model we can get a better perspective by a little adjustment here, raising or lowering the roof, by extending the eaves—to give it graceful lines. You don't want your cabin to look like a garage when it is finished.

You will become so thoroughly familiar with every piece of log or lumber—its dimension and fitting—used in your cabin you will approach the real building with confidence and sound enjoyment.

Build your miniature cabin one inch to the foot. In the winter in your workshop, you will find this an ideal hobby. Whittle the logs of soft white pine about three-quarters of an inch in diameter. Use thin packing boxes for lumber and cut to size. Your hardware store will supply you with one-quarter-inch and one-half-inch brads for nails. Leave the roof removable, so you can look inside and plan for the rooms. Build tiny book-racks, lockers, beds, et cetera, your table and rustic chairs, and build them to scale. Have the family check each item with you. Rearrange doors and windows to your liking. Check space and, if unsatisfactory, make changes. Then you won't be disappointed or wish you had done it differently. When erecting your cabin, take the miniature along. It will serve as a blueprint, or better.

Of course, the easier way is to hire an architect and contractor, but more than half of the fun is building Your Cabin in the Woods, from the planning to the building, with your own hands. It will be really yours. It's what you put into it of yourself that will really make it a part of you.

Let's Go
to Work

WHEN you really get serious about building a Cabin in the Woods, you will very quickly envision rather definite ideas of your own. By all means, hold on to them. The ideas are usually larger and surrounded with more grandeur, more spacious quarters, added acres often beyond your finances to carry them through. Then comes the paring down process to fit the pocketbook. At this point, you may welcome suggestions, but you do not want to be told, "This is the only way," or "This is the only kind of a cabin." After all, this is your project. It will mean little when finished unless it has your personality, your own innovations, your own architecture built into the sum total. Perhaps these offerings may stimulate your thinking and planning. They may save you some of the errors commonly made. Lengthy descriptions have been avoided purposely. There is no one way. Your own aptitude, your own peculiar kind of initiative, and the ability to use your hands, together with native intelligence (horse sense) precludes anyone from trespassing with the final answer. So if I can be your helper, let's go to work.

Your "treasure chest" is really your tool chest full of sharp tools. You can save yourself endless trouble and add to your enjoyment by building

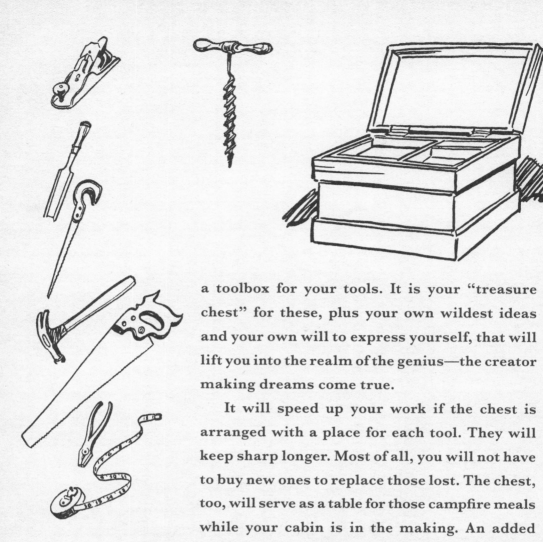

a toolbox for your tools. It is your "treasure chest" for these, plus your own wildest ideas and your own will to express yourself, that will lift you into the realm of the genius—the creator making dreams come true.

It will speed up your work if the chest is arranged with a place for each tool. They will keep sharp longer. Most of all, you will not have to buy new ones to replace those lost. The chest, too, will serve as a table for those campfire meals while your cabin is in the making. An added cushion will make it a part of your cabin furniture.

Cabin Tools— Keep 'em Sharp

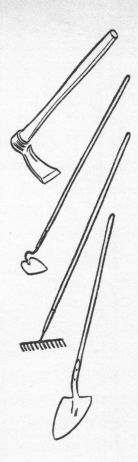

THERE is nothing, in my experience, more trying, more time wasting, and disheartening than to attempt to carve a turkey, repair a door, or build a cabin with dull or inadequate tools.

A tool chest and a workshop will always be a part of your cabin craft—so prepare for it. Stock the essential implements you will need if you are to get real satisfaction from your efforts. Good tools need protection—a roof—and a lock. If your building occurs on weekends and scattered days, a small shed is a good investment. The shed may later serve as a chicken coop, a woodshed, or for storage. A tent is probably sufficient coverage if you can stay on the job until it is complete.

Either build or buy a workbench with a vise attached. You must have the vise to grip firmly the boards upon which you want to work. Your tool chest should contain hammers, a level, screwdrivers, square, chalk, a soft pencil or two, tough string for plumb lines and an adequate plane, a sturdy auger that will

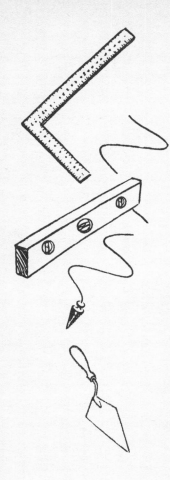

bore holes at least one and a half inches in diameter. Add a carborundum stone for fine edge sharpening. Put in a supply of nails of needed sizes, weights, and lengths for each particular bit of construction. Splitting pieces of wood because of improper nails or screws is disappointing—and a waste of time.

Besides these smaller essentials, you will need saws, a reliable jackknife, a draw-shave for shaping rustic furniture and trimming logs, and an axe—more about this king of tools elsewhere. For ground work, a post-hole digger is a great time saver. A pickaxe, a crowbar, shovels, rake and hoe, and grub axe.

Now something to keep the tools sharp. An old-fashioned grindstone goes well with your cabin craft. On a rainy day, I get the grindstone working and sharpen my axes. This done, I get my collection of jackknives, bowie knives, and—just to keep in right with the kitchen folk—the butcher knives and kitchen knives. There is nothing like a grindstone for really sharpening steel. The water dripping from the can above prevents overheating the metal. I'm sure you will now defend the emery or carborundum wheel. I have one connected with power. It is good for rough work, but, too often, I have burned a good piece of steel by

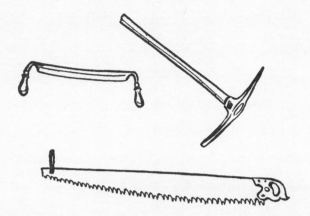

overheating. Once burned, the life is gone from the steel. To grind an axe or knife properly takes practice—a steady hand and patience. Edge tools should be held against the stone at an angle so the sharpest part of the edge barely touches the stone. As you wear the rough high spots down toward the fine edge, your blade will even up.

The flat fine carborundum stone is most valuable for the final finishing. To give your tool its final keen edge, use an eight-inch flat carborundum stone.

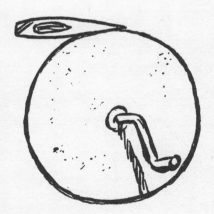

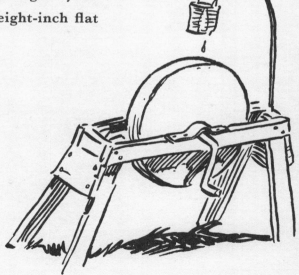

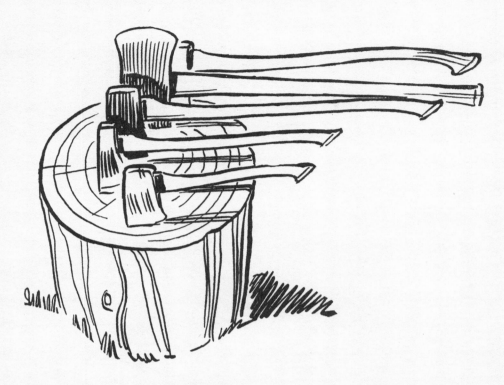

THE AXE

Now, if you are a city person who goes to the woods for weekends, who has most of his work done for him, you won't need an axe. For the real cabin builder, the axe is his best friend. With an axe, you can fashion a rough cabin or hunting shelter; with an axe, you can build traps and snares to catch wild animals for food; with an axe you can blaze your way through dense woods—notching a return trail; with an axe, you can cut firewood for cooking and for warmth. Without an axe, I should feel helpless in the woods. It is the first "must" on my list of tools.

At this point, if you are a novice in axemanship, you might expect further instruction on how to handle an axe. Any expert would agree with me, such written directions would be bad teaching. Here is a craft that cannot be gained from books. The skill must be handed down by one who knows—it must be learned in the doing.

Many books have been written on how to play golf. They may serve for winter sport beside a fireplace. But, to benefit from real instruction, the amateur still goes to the golf course—asks the guidance of a golf "pro." The "pro" knows the why and how of grips, stance, and position and teaches right out on the course. So also in learning the use of an axe. Find the farmer who cuts his own wood from his woodlot or the lumberjack or craftsman who earns his salt with an axe. Either one will say, "Well, come along to the woodpile—we'll cut firewood while we are learning." This will result in added skill for you—and more wood for the woodpile—and you won't have to pay five dollars an hour for this most practical instruction.

As your skill improves, you will not be satisfied with one axe. I have seventeen in actual use. A bit of a hobby? Yes—but each axe has a special purpose. They differ in shape, weight, and length. They range from the dainty light axe for fine work to the broad axe used in pioneer days for squaring logs to build beams and block houses. The broad axe is little used today, but I wouldn't part with mine.

Some axes are for cutting, others for splitting. Cutting-axes must be sharp to be effective. Keep them sharp—razor sharp—and you will respect them. I once saw a lumberjack in northern Wisconsin shave his partner with a two-bitted axe—not for the sake of the shave but to demonstrate what he meant by a razor-sharp edge on his axe.

An old tree stump provides a center for sport and healthy exercise for my guests when we play throw the hatchet. I have four old axes for this purpose. The object of the game is to throw the hatchet twenty or thirty feet so it will stick into the old stump. It's not at all difficult. Throw the axe overhead with the blade pointing forward. The axe must make a complete revolution before it hits the stump. So if you miss, stand a little farther back. Vary your position until you connect. Each axe and each contestant's force vary.

No camp is complete without one or more axes.

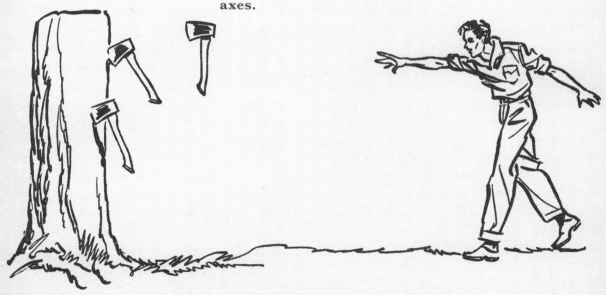

KNIVES

Next to the axe in usefulness is the woodsman's knife. In this day and age, we are inclined to think of the pocketknife as a dainty pearl-handled affair for sharpening pencils and cutting string on packages. No true woodsman would tolerate such a tool.

Knife collecting, I must confess, is quite as much a hobby of mine as my hoarding of axes. A few of them are rare antiques. The case of one is made from a deer's foot—hair and all. Another, it is claimed, saved the life of my grandfather when faced with a bear. Caught without a gun, grandfather fought it out with his knife. Scared and bruised, he was saved by the knife.

A woodsman and cabin builder needs both a jackknife in his pocket and a stout bowie knife in a sheath attached to his belt. Hunters, too, need this sharp bowie knife, for a deer, after being shot, should at once be bled and dressed.

In my collection are knives from three to eighteen inches in length. I have a set of fine carving tools, each of them razor sharp. It is fun to show your skill with a roast beef or a well-browned fowl. If your knife is sharp, the carving is quite simple—just steady the roast with a large fork and draw your knife back and forth. With a little practice, you can cut roast beef in even, thick or paper-thin, slices. For

69

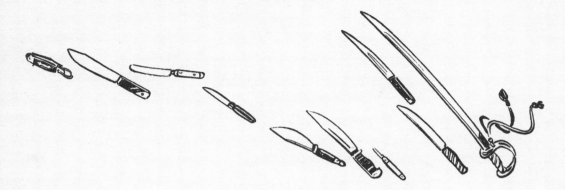

fowl, I prefer a short thin blade. It is easier to find and separate the joints. A longer thin blade should be at hand for carving the slices of white breast meat.

In our family—as in most families—are swords from past wars. We had several: commanders' swords three feet long, bayonets, a fencing saber, a dirk, and short dagger for close-in engagements. These tools were designed for killing men. They are refashioned now into implements for peacetime pursuits—for carving and for pruning.

The commander's sword was a piece of excellent steel. Using my emery wheel and grindstone, I cut it in two, regrinding the blades into fine carving knives that are among my prized cutting tools.

Good steel is sometimes hard to get. If you are one of those who must have a really good knife of the best tempered steel—and are willing to do the necessary grinding—reconvert an old steel file. Steel files must be made of the best tempered steel. They can be ground to the shape and size desired. A twelve-inch file can be ground into a perfect carving knife.

The story is told of two ancient kings who demonstrated to each other their skill with the sword. The first king, a giant in size, drew forth his heavy powerful weapon. With one mighty blow, he severed an iron bar one inch thick. The second king drew forth his slender, delicate, razor-sharp blade. He drew it across a feather pillow—splitting the case with such hair-precision no bit of down was spilled. The moral of this bedtime story is not important here. For me, I prefer the delicate skill that comes from sharp well-balanced tools, handled by those who appreciate how to use them.

Nails

CHOOSING the right kind and size of nails to be driven into wood is as important as knowing what ingredients go into a cake, or which golf club to use for making a particular shot. The purpose of the nail is to hold two pieces of wood together. If the pieces of wood are thick, i.e., nailing two pieces of two-by-four together, then longer and stouter nails are required. If to nail two one-inch boards together, then a smaller nail will do.

There are cut nails, common wire nails,

horseshoe nails, finishing nails, penny nails, and others. For our purpose in the use of nails that will deal mostly with joinery and carpentry, there are three kinds of nails to be considered. They are called penny nails, box nails, and finishing nails.

Penny nails run from two-penny to sixty-penny nails. A two-penny is one inch in length, a three-penny is one and one-quarter inches long, and so on up to a sixty-penny, which is about seven inches in length.

The penny nail is a heavy nail with a sturdy shank that can be driven hard with a heavy hammer without bending. Never choose a nail longer than the thickness of the wood you want to nail together. If you choose a nail longer, so it sticks out on the other side, you are wasting that piece of the nail; but, more than this, you add nothing to the holding strength of the nail. It should be buried thoroughly into the two pieces of wood you are binding together. To turn over the piece of protruding nail indeed locks the nail into the wood, but, in so doing, there is danger of partly driving it back and your boards are not tight fitting.

Box nails run about the same size as penny nails, but are thinner and for finer work.

Lastly, finishing nails are for cabinetwork. These have small heads, which, when driven into the wood, can be sunk deeper with a nail set so no part of the nail is above the surface of the wood.

With the last stroke of the hammer, which finally plants the nail in your board, care must be taken to hit gently so as not to injure the grain of the wood, if you want to produce fine workmanship.

Building Rules You May Not Violate

Anyone with a general working knowledge of tools can build his own cabin, if he follows a few simple but fundamental rules:

1. Set foundation or piers below the frost line. If in deep woods, freezing is not as severe. Bank your cabin in the fall with leaves.

2. Set the foundation both level and truly square. This will save endless trouble as building develops. Triangles of three, four, and five feet will give you a large square; also six, eight, and ten feet. Here is how you do it. Drive a stake (A) firmly into the ground at the corner of your planned cabin. Mark a

cross (X) on the top. From the center of this cross measure off exactly three feet along the side of your cabin and then drive the second stake (B). At right angles to this line and starting again from the first stake (A), measure off four feet and drive a stake (C). This done, measure from (B) to (C). It must measure exactly five feet and you then have a right angle triangle with (A) at the base. If it does not measure exactly five feet, move stake (C) until it does. Your whole structure will reveal good lines by the care you exercise in the use of the plane, plumb line, or level and the square.

3. Square, level, and plumb tell the truth. Never guess.

4. Sharp tools will speed up the work.

5. Provide for thorough drainage about the cabin.

6. Build from a plan, not memory. Don't rush it through in a weekend. Take a month, six months, or a year. Your greatest pleasure will be in the building and your greatest enjoyment will be in the satisfaction of a comfortable, snug, and well-built cabin.

7. If in doubt, seek expert advice.

Land Cost

LAND can be secured at surprisingly low cost or at low rental. Poor farm land, i.e., land cut deep with ravines, is of little value to the farmer and ideal for our purpose, especially if there are trees, bushes, and shrubs.

Over the past thirty years, I have traveled the length and breadth of this country. Whether New York State, Florida, the Rockies, or the prairie lands of the southwest, there is an unlimited quantity of land available. More than this, it can be purchased inexpensively.

The trouble with most of us is we want so many feet frontage on a lake or stream or ocean. Or we want the highest hill for a view. For these, of course, we must pay. Let us think simply. A bit of land, say five acres, off the main highway, a lovely view to the south, a real vista after removing one or two trees and bushes. The land is rough and rocky, but this is no obstacle. It's a challenge, for here we shall build a rock garden, trails, an out-of-door rustic stove for picnic suppers.

You will find plenty of land for your purpose "off the beaten path," and it will be within your means. If you do not wish to own the land, you can work out a rental arrangement, say, for five, ten, or fifteen years.

If you live in a big city, the distance to travel will be greater. Do not cast the idea of a Cabin in the Woods aside just because you may not own an automobile. It still can be done even if you have to take the bus or trolley or train. It will help you grow strong and more resourceful. Yes—it will increase your earning power. Some day you may have that auto, also a trailer.

Cabin Cost

THAT all depends on how lavish you wish to be and on your own resources—how many rooms, how much land. Remember, the purpose of this book is to help the novice who wants to play a big part in building his own cabin—who wants to be resourceful.

If you hire your labor instead of doing most of it yourself, or buy rustic furniture instead of creating it out of woods material, or are in a hurry to complete Your Cabin in the Woods, then, of course, costs will mount. A good slogan to keep in mind is "Utilize all natural resources. Do it yourself. Take time." Even hinges, door locks, coat hangers, shelves, shingles, stone steps, and slab floors need nothing more than a few tools, the natural resources at your disposal, and the will to make it your own handicraft.

If this is your first cabin-building experience, avoid larger cabins than here suggested, for both carpentering and structural problems will present themselves that are not included in these plates. A big cabin needs additional reinforcing, heavier timber, supports, et cetera. You will become discouraged. Our ancestors, the old pioneers, built small cabins and lived in them. You will lose the lore and spirit of a Cabin in the Woods with a big house. Again, a good carpenter is not necessarily a good log cabin builder. Different technique is involved, and you gain this technique through experience. You will later want to build another and will benefit by your first experience.

Logs for Your Cabin

CHOOSE softwoods rather than hardwoods for your first experience—hemlock, bass, pine, even poplar works up easily into logs. By all means, avoid working with oak logs unless you are thoroughly familiar with this wood. It is "temperamental." I have seen it, after it was thoroughly dried, seasoned, squared, and fitted into place, change form a year after the cabin was built. It will twist slightly like a barber pole, even to lifting your cabin at one corner and leaving big cracks to patch from year to year. But that's another story.

Speaking of green softwood logs—it will pay you to remove the bark. Use a draw-shave. Insects get under the bark and may cause you much annoyance. There are methods of preserving the bark, but I still favor stripping the logs. It will give you a clean cabin. Old cedar telephone poles redressed are recommended, if you can get them. They are dry and ready for use. Dressing old telephone poles is fun, and will give most satisfying results. The grain in cedar logs is straight. With a sharp axe, dig in about one inch all around. The wood will come off in long strips—two, three, and four feet long. After the rough axe work, finish and smooth off with a draw-shave. Your logs will look like new timber and the sweet smell of cedar will reward you for your added effort.

Fourteen logs with an average thickness of eight or nine inches and twenty-six feet long will build a cabin twelve by fourteen feet up to fourteen by sixteen feet, depending upon the number of doors and windows.

Pile the logs far enough apart and crisscross

to give them all the air possible for drying. If the logs are green, it is best to allow them to dry several months before using. When hauling your logs to your cabin site, place them equally on either side of the planned building. This will save unnecessary loads after the logs are sawed up. Remove knots and burls to have logs as nearly straight and smooth as possible.

Tie Your Cabin Together

There are three important places to bind your cabin:

1. After placing the sill logs, which rest on the foundation and should, of course, run parallel to each other, place your floor joists running at right angles to the sills. The log sills should be dug out to accommodate the two-inch-by-six-inch floor joists and then nailed in securely. This binds your floor both ways after you lay a double floor.

2. The next place to tie in is at the plates, which rest on top of your logs and corner studs and form the base for your roof construction to fasten to. Plates should be two inches by six inches, laid double and overlapped at every

corner to bind and leave no weak spots. Logs may be used as plates and they, too, should overlap at corners and then be bolted together as well as spiked to corner studs.

3. The third important tie-in is in the roof rafters, for a hip roof will spread, especially under heavy snows, and so roof rafters should be bound together to hold your roof rigid. In northern zones where there is a great deal of snow, more rafters should be added. The floor joists should be of two-inch-by-six-inch lumber supported in the middle, and the roof rafters for the size of cabin here suggested can be of two inches by six inches, but preferably of saplings dressed and trimmed— all about four or five inches in diameter.

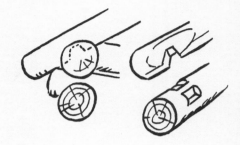

LOGS BEVELED TOWARD WINDOW

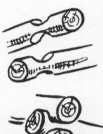

Notching Your Logs

NOTCHING logs is a craft one does not learn merely by reading books. Notching logs so they fit together snugly is an art all in itself. It belongs to the pioneer skills, to the woodsman, to the one intimately acquainted with an axe—more than this, with the broad axe, the pewee, the cant hook.

If you want a cabin true to the pioneer background, it will be of the notched-log construction and you will need to find a backwoodsman who has mastered the art of delicately swinging an axe. He will teach you more in a day than you can learn from a dozen books. As has been said often, "Theory without practice is empty and practice without theory is deadly." Combine the two and you will acquire a technique that is workable. Only then will you be on your own.

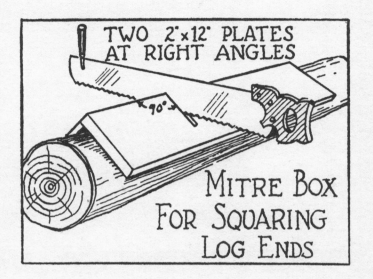

TWO 2"x12" PLATES AT RIGHT ANGLES

90°

MITRE BOX FOR SQUARING LOG ENDS

MAINE-WOODS METHOD OF BINDING LOGS AT CORNERS

The old-fashioned method of notching logs is more costly as it requires at least four additional feet on each log and, unless expertly done, will be a disappointment to you.

The Maine-Woods Method saves time, labor, and material, and gives you very satisfactory results. After the foundation logs or sills have been placed and squared, toenail a double or "V" studding at each corner—that is, a two-inch-by-six-inch stud spiked at right angles to a two-inch-by-eight-inch, so the two are "V" shaped. (Use six-penny spikes.) The outside will measure eight inches; the inside, six inches. Place this on the sill at the corner so the mouth of the "V" faces outside. (At bay window intersections, the mouth of the "V" faces inside.) A "V" studding now placed at every corner of the cabin and carefully toenailed, should be topped with a double plate or two two-inch-by-eight-inch running all around, or a log overlapping. Be sure the two-inch-by eight-inch plates bind or overlap at all points.

Cut logs with care to fit exactly between your "V" studding or doorjamb and windows, then spike with six-penny spikes through the stud wall and into the end of the log. Use at least three spikes for each end of the log. Pack spaces between the end of the log and studding with oakum. Keep logs spaced at least one inch apart to provide for generous chinking.

Cabin Detail

HERE is a complete picture story of the Maine-woods cabin construction from the foundation to roof rafters.

Concrete foundation down below the frost line; base logs anchored by bolts to the foundation.

Next, we have "V" studs at all corners with logs spiked at the ends; log plates properly notched, bolted, and anchored; finally, roof log rafters to complete the log frame.

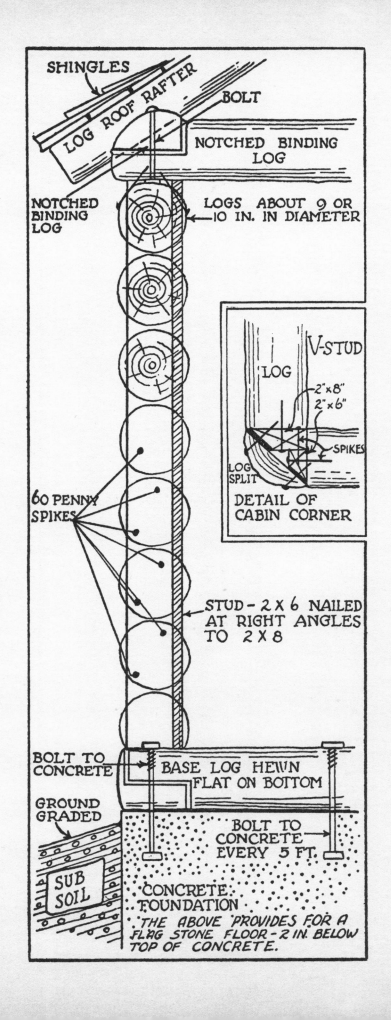

SHINGLES

LOG ROOF RAFTER

BOLT

NOTCHED BINDING LOG

NOTCHED BINDING LOG

LOGS ABOUT 9 OR 10 IN. IN DIAMETER

V-STUD

LOG

2"×8"

2"×6"

SPIKES

LOG SPLIT

DETAIL OF CABIN CORNER

60 PENNY SPIKES

STUD – 2 X 6 NAILED AT RIGHT ANGLES TO 2 X 8

BOLT TO CONCRETE

BASE LOG HEWN FLAT ON BOTTOM

GROUND GRADED

BOLT TO CONCRETE EVERY 5 FT.

SUB SOIL

CONCRETE FOUNDATION

THE ABOVE PROVIDES FOR A FLAG STONE FLOOR – 2 IN. BELOW TOP OF CONCRETE.

The insert presents in detail the "V" stud construction.

Study these plates until you are thoroughly familiar with every detail. Build your miniature from these plates. This type of log cabin construction is really very economical as against overlapping logs. It will give you a sturdy building "tight as a drum."

Windows, Doors, and Gables

ACCORDING to the thickness of your logs, build your own window frames out of two-inch-by-six-inch or two-inch-by-eight-inch lumber and place windows in double, so they overlap and slide past each other. Place strips on the outside and inside of the window, so they may slide back and forth. This removes hinges and the inconvenience of having windows inside a room when they are open. As you bring your logs up to the desired height, place your whole window frame on the log and build around it. Be sure your frame is exactly squared. Do this by keeping it braced both ways on the frame. You can purchase from your wood dealer almost any size windows you

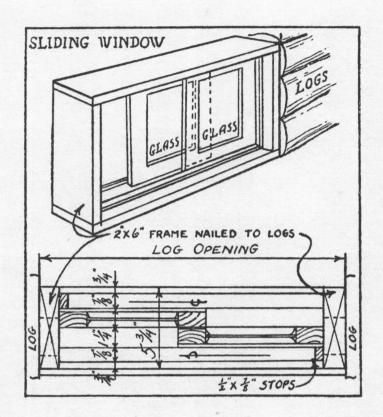

SLIDING WINDOW

LOGS

GLASS GLASS

2"x6" FRAME NAILED TO LOGS
LOG OPENING

LOG

LOG

3/4"

1/8"

1/2"

1/8"

3/8"

5 3/4"

1/2" x 7/8" STOPS

wish. Your cabin is likely to be dark unless you provide one window large enough to give ample light. There is no need for feeling cooped up. It costs a little more, but it is worth it.

Be sure to put a small opening in the gables of Your Cabin in the Woods—both ends. These are for ventilators. You can control these by a shutter-string. Screen them on the outside. Leave them slightly open when you leave your cabin and you will find it sweet and fresh smelling when you return. On the coldest night, you can sleep comfortably with plenty of fresh air by opening these two vents, and by the dead air that will be drawn out by your fireplace.

Build your doorframes out of two-inch-by-six-inch or two-inch-by-eight-inch lumber and place strips inside the doorjamb against which to fit the door. The doorjamb serves also as a stud. Nail through it to hold your log.

Drainage and Grading

CERTAINLY you should not choose a marshy spot for your cabin. It is self-evident there would be dampness, wet floors, rheumatism, the doctor.

Choose first a knoll or high ground that pitches down from your cabin site. Rain, but especially melting snow, will flow away from your cabin. This is a rule you may not change if you want a dry cabin.

Of course, you want your cabin to nestle into its surroundings. Give it, however, at least eighteen inches elevation above the natural ground and have it drain down and away from your building on all sides. The ground dug out from the foundation, or should you decide to dig a cellar, should be thrown outside the foundation. You won't have to dig the foundation so deep if you raise the level without.

To do a really fine job, especially if you use a flagstone floor within, is to lay a three-inch tile at the bottom of the foundation on the outside. Be sure it pitches downward from one side of the building all around to the point where it drains down the hillside.

Upper and Lower Bunks Converted into Couches

BY building in upper and lower bunks, the upper bunk can be hinged. Drop the front of the upper bunk to form the backrest of the couch with the lower bunk.

Painting and Preservatives

AS you read more into this subject, you will find many recommendations. The old pioneer had no paint or stain and his building stood the test of time. Window frames, windowsills, doorjambs, and doors can be painted or, better, stained.

Beautiful effects can be had by working out a weather-stain color. After your logs have thoroughly dried, it will be a far better time to stain with preservatives.

Chinking

CHINKING between logs will make a cabin warm, clean, and dry. It should be carefully done. It pays in the end. Logs must be dried thoroughly. Plaster with sand, four parts; lime, one-half to one part; white cement, one part. If spaces of one inch or more occur between logs, fill in with small branches nailed to the top and bottom logs, inside and out. Don't be too sparing with the plaster. Wide plaster spaces will brighten the room, too. Plaster well if you want a warm cabin. The plaster on the outside should not touch or meet the plaster on the inside, for the dead air space makes the best nonconductor. To make plaster hold between the logs, drive nails as far in as possible into logs both up and down near the middle of the crack—many of them—say every three or four inches—old nails, crooked nails. Another good method is to nail in woven wire

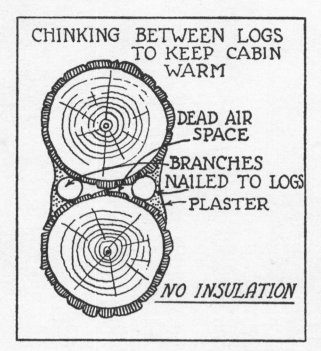

CHINKING BETWEEN LOGS TO KEEP CABIN WARM

DEAD AIR SPACE

BRANCHES NAILED TO LOGS

PLASTER

NO INSULATION

or hardware cloth, one-quarter-inch mesh. Cut the hardware cloth in strips about three inches wide; fold lengthwise in a slight "V" shape and drive in between the logs and nail to the upper or lower log. This is not absolutely necessary, but gives added strength. Dead air space makes the perfect nonconductor.

Better to chink with moss if logs are not thoroughly dry or leave unchinked until dry. Lime, one part; sand, three parts; wood ashes, twenty-five parts; salt, two parts, all thoroughly mixed with dry moss will serve well for a hunter's lodge. The ashes tend to keep vermin away.

When chinking is complete, if any light spots show through a door or window jamb, caulk it with tarred hemp, oakum, or moss. The tar smell soon disappears. Be especially careful to chink between the ground or sill log above before laying a floor.

Indoor
Fire

Fireplace Magic

IT is a simple thing to talk about a glowing fireplace. To achieve one takes skill, plus a few tricks up your sleeve. The ash bed is important. The kind of wood and the placing of the logs determine your success. The only thermostat is the fire builder himself. If he learns the secret of its magic, he can make of his fire making a fine art, shading it, highlighting it, coloring it with craftsmanship that need not depend on chemicals from a package or bottle.

Let's learn the art from scratch. Those unacquainted with fireplace craft will clean out and scour the fire bed, leaving it empty, clean, naked. I have discovered the main reason. They desire a clean and tidy setting. So do I. Ashes can add rather than detract from the beauty and efficiency of your fire. Today we desecrate a fire by throwing into it cigar and cigarette butts, trash, and paper. These seldom burn in entirety, and, if they do, leave a black char that is most unsightly. It might seem unnecessary to say food waste should never enter into this symbol of family life. A fireplace that is an incinerator would have to be cleaned. A fireplace that centers the warmth and light and friendliness of a group of fireplace lovers will never be so desecrated.

A fireplace without a deep cushion of ashes is like a bed without a mattress. Ashes form the soft warm bed for the next fire. Without it, the logs won't burn correctly. The mat of ashes should be six inches deep at the back wall of your fireplace. They will be white and clean if you become a master of your art and burn only hardwood.

So, first, as you build your fire, rake the ashes back so they slant upward from the hearth's front to the six-inch depth at the back of the fire wall. You need no grate or andirons. A bed of ashes is the real need. In the center of your fireplace, build a small tepee of kindling, dry tinder bits, preferably full of pitch. At right angles, one on either side, lay two three- or four-inch sticks of wood running from front to back. Now lay a thick backlog, say ten inches, way in the back on the sticks; next, forward, a smaller log in thickness, but not touching. Then, a still smaller log and so on to the hearth's edge. Air currents, which create correct draft, travel along the outside or ends of these logs, flowing up and in between them. A diagonal log placed on top of this pile will give added pull to the flame. Your fire is ready for lighting. As the coals form and the under-logs burn through and allow the fire to settle into the coal and ash bed, they will not need to be replaced, as the flames themselves give added impetus. If you want your fireplace full of lively flame—I don't mean just a flickering glow, but a burst of light and warmth—continue to add logs diagonally or thrust into the crevices, upright smaller pieces—"ticklers" I call them. Abe Lincoln did his studying by such a light.

Your choice of woods depends upon the purpose and the mood for which the fire is designed. Some woods make a crackling fire. Others throw out showers of sparks. Still others burn slowly and leave a deep bed of coals. Hemlock, pine, and other softwoods are good for kindling, but burn out quickly and leave a dark ash. Beech, maple, elm, ash, and hickory are tops. Oak and pitch pine will burn well together. They leave a bed of glowing coals and, when spent, a white ash. Any of these hardwoods can be used for broiling steaks. A deep bed of coals is essential to any fireplace cooking.

Try birch wood for a fire of welcome. It sputters, crackles, seems to say to your five o'clock tea guest, "Come in. Warm up a bit. Draw up a chair." Birch doesn't last long, but it is sprightly while it burns. I keep a small stock of this rollicking, laughing wood for such special occasions.

Now let me tell you about the choicest of all fire logs, if you want a quiet, colorful fire for the late evening—for the deeper, more silent moods. It neither spits nor sparkles. It throws blue, red, green, yellow, and purple flames and all the shades and colors in between. It inspires close companionship. This special, magic wood is just your old apple tree from the orchard. It is gnarled, covered with buds, often sprouting twigs. It's a tough old tree. Even when its inside is hollow, it keeps right on growing—giving shade and apples. The very hollowness adds to your fire magic. Set it up, chimney fashion, and watch the glow and constant change of color. Watch the "fire fairies" climb out of its heart and soar upward with the smoke. I sometimes fancy the old tree is remembering and sharing with us the earlier glory of its pink and cream blossoms, the human romances that bloomed in its deep green shade, the fulfillment of its green and scarlet fruit. As a tree, the apple is a romantic, attracting young and old. As firewood, it is an artist of color that warms the hands, the heart—the soul.

The overnight backlog is indeed a part of your fireplace craft. You can keep your log burning

all night. If properly buried it will greet you in the morning as a solid log of glowing coals. Just before going to bed take your shovel and rake forward from the back wall of your fireplace all coals and ashes. Dig down deep through the six inches of ashes a place to hold a ten-inch log. After dropping the log into this hollow, cover all of it with the rest of your coals and ashes. Bury it until you can see no part of the log for coals and ashes. Now place your screen in front of the hearth for protection from sparks. Behold, tomorrow morning you will find your log of red-hot coals. Our pioneer fathers did this always; especially in the days when there were no matches and fires were built by rubbing sticks, or with flint on steel. On the mantle shelf stood a jar of long slender sticks about pencil thickness and of pitchy wood. These served as matches for grandfather's pipe, or for lighting candles.

In my boyhood days I used to watch, fascinated, the sparks that would ignite on the black charred fireplace wall when the coals were low. These sparks would not flame up, just creep through the gathered creosote—building fantastic shapes of floating clouds, birds, animals, and, finally, as if by magic, disappearing.

There really is magic in a fireplace.

Fireplaces Successfully Built by the Novice

WORKING with brick and mortar is fascinating. It will give you a thorough respect for this craft. Fireplace building is hard work, back breaking, yet worth all the effort in the pleasure a glowing hearth will give. Diligent application and any handyman with a few tools and the will to "stick" can succeed. Our ancestors had to rely on their own skill or develop it. It's just a part of the American spirit.

First, let us make it attractive—simple lines, stones from the field, fit together like patterns in a flagstone floor. Flat sandstones or limestones work up best. Fashioning stones from the field for your fireplace will present some problems and an occasional "frustration." With a little practice and perseverance, however, you will suddenly discover you can split a stone with precision. You will experience a new thrill. This, then, is learning by doing and in the doing you will find yourself tired, muscles a bit sore, hands hardened and rough, but you will say over and over again, "I did it. I have it. I know it." You will go to bed wholesomely tired, but eager to get off to an early start in the morning, to work again on your fireplace.

Use natural material, if available, before resorting to brick. Be sure, however, to line your fireplace with firebrick.

Do not attempt a large fireplace if it is your first experiment. The two fireplaces shown are workable. One is different, raised fourteen inches above the floor, with a shelf that makes an excellent space for cooking and will save your back. It warms the body and the room—not just the shins.

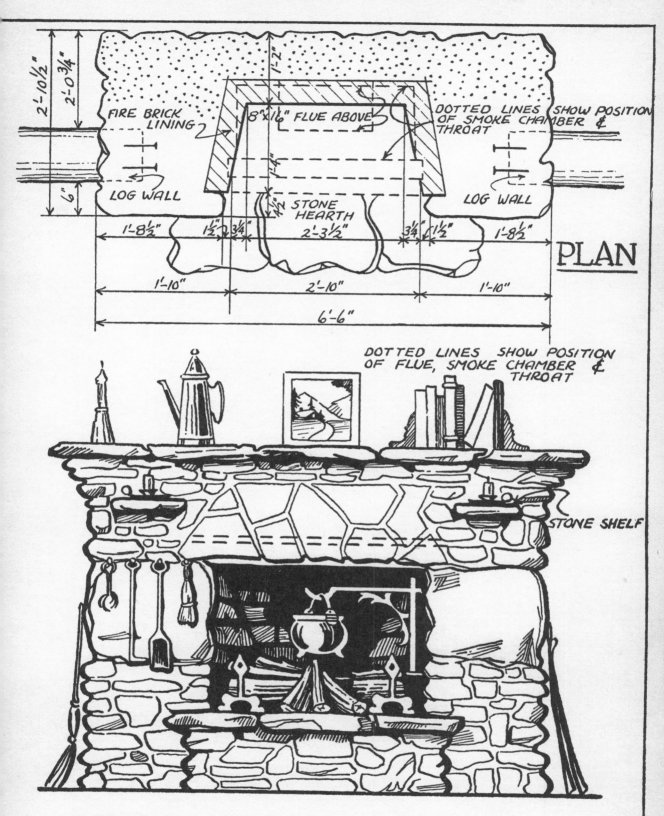

PLAN

DETAIL OF FIREPLACE
WITH RAISED HEARTH

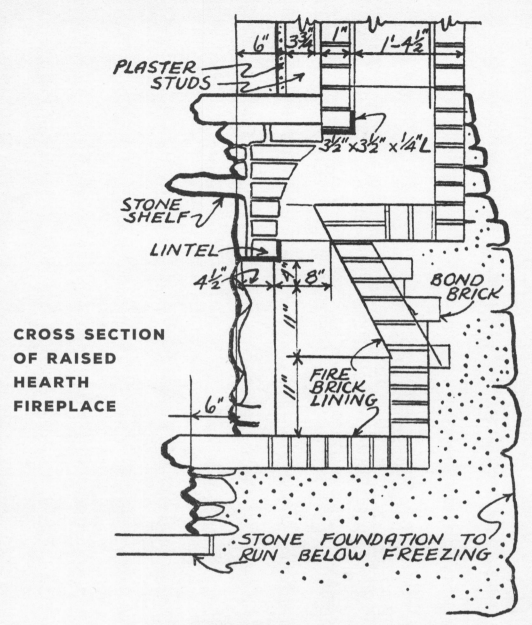

PLASTER
STUDS

6" 3¾" 1" 1'-4½"

3½" x 3½" x ¼" L

STONE
SHELF

LINTEL

4½" 4" 8"

BOND
BRICK

**CROSS SECTION
OF RAISED
HEARTH
FIREPLACE**

6"

FIRE
BRICK
LINING

STONE FOUNDATION TO
RUN BELOW FREEZING

IMPORTANT

Build your fireplace at the end of the room away from doors, to give snugness and avoid drafts. Your fireplace will give warmth, a welcome glow, and throw shadows. Do not expect a fireplace to keep a cabin warm in sub-zero weather. Place a wood-burning stove at the opposite end of the room. Run a smokestack through the roof with a metal collar. You will then be between two fires and warmed both "fore and aft."

SMALL BRICK FIREPLACE

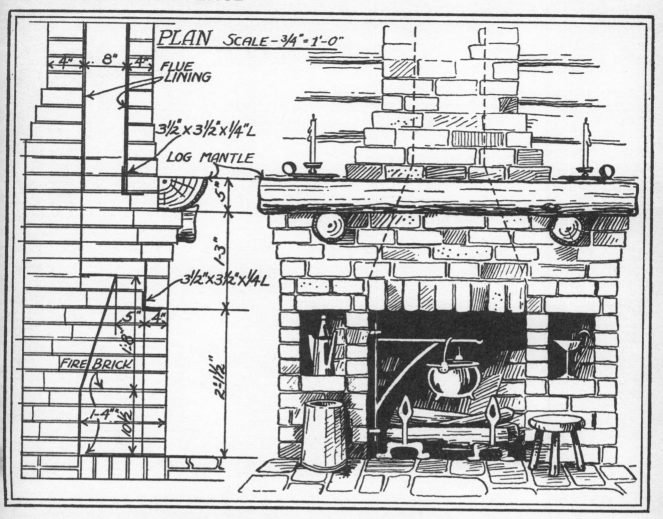

PLAN SCALE - 3/4" = 1'-0"

4" · 8" · 4"

FLUE LINING

3½" x 3½" x ¼" L

LOG MANTLE

5"

1'-3"

3½" x 3½" x ¼" L

5" · 4"

8"

FIRE BRICK

1'-4" · 10½"

2'-1½"

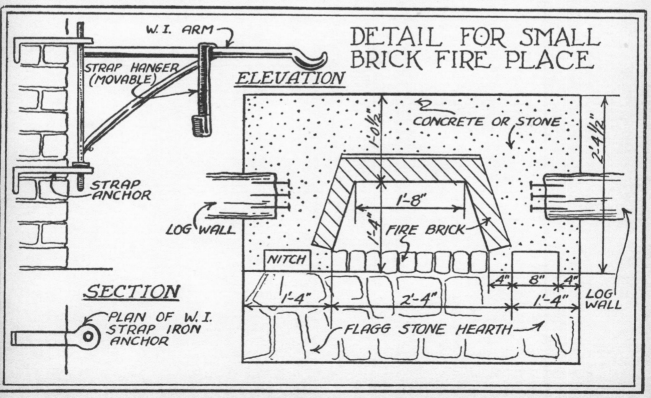

DETAIL FOR SMALL BRICK FIRE PLACE

ELEVATION

W. I. ARM

STRAP HANGER (MOVABLE)

STRAP ANCHOR

LOG WALL

CONCRETE OR STONE

1'-0½"

2'-4½"

1'-8"

1'-4"

FIRE BRICK

NITCH

4" · 8" · 4"

1'-4" · 2'-4" · 1'-4"

LOG WALL

SECTION

PLAN OF W. I. STRAP IRON ANCHOR

FLAGG STONE HEARTH

THE "WHY" OF FIREPLACES
THAT BURN WELL

It is tragic to see so many lovely cabins spoiled by smoking fireplaces. A good many fireplaces are built by people who do not understand the first principles of fireplace construction. Books on the subject are available at your library; also, the United States Department of Agriculture Farmers' Bulletin No. 1649 treats this subject at length. If measurements here given are followed, your fireplace will not smoke, but will burn perfectly, keeping logs burning overnight, and will be a joy in your cabin.

After your fireplace has dried out for a few days, light your first really great fire. What a thrill! It works. Call in the family, your friends. Celebrate.

If it smokes, sit alone and study it. Watch the air currents. Light a bundle of sticks or newspaper and hold it at the upper corners of the opening. If the flue does not draw the flame and smoke, then there is something wrong about the throat. Get your chisel and dig inside on either side of the throat above the lintel. Here is the greatest possibility of trouble. If you are sure the flue is in correct measured relationship to the opening, you really can't go very wrong. After you have adjusted here and there until the fireplace really burns, you will approach the next fireplace with added confidence and will have good results.

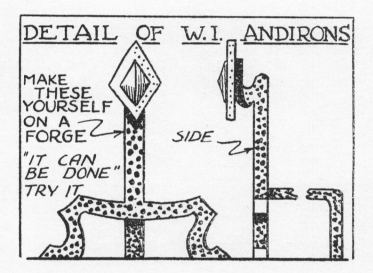

TOOLS

Level, plumb line, mixing box two by four feet and ten inches deep, hoe, trowel, mason's hammer, chalk line, square, shovel.

MATERIALS

Stones or bricks, sand, gravel, cement, lime, nails, chalk, iron lintel arch support, eight inches longer than the width of the opening (angle iron lintel will not sag), one hundred firebricks, twenty-five pounds of fireclay, pothooks, pothook supports.

HOW TO PROCEED

Build the foundation the full size of the fireplace, two feet to four feet and six inches below ground level, according to your freezing line; fill in with concrete and stones.

Rest the floor joists on the fireplace's foundation. Fill in with concrete between the joists to floor level, unless you plan a flagstone floor.

Build the fireplace by levels—i.e., do not build up one side, then the other. If you add a four-inch stone on one corner, bring the rest of the fireplace up likewise, then add the next tier.

Make it rough. If one stone protrudes, good, but bring the one above it back true with your plumb line.

Rake out the mortar about one inch deep between joists. This will give an aged or weathered appearance. Keep your mortar stiff, i.e., not too much water.

A false hearth is cheaper, but not so sturdy. Build your hearth the full width of the fireplace.

If in a log cabin, the fireplace foundation must be deeper front to back to allow for the thickness of the logs.

Bring the foundation to within six inches of the floor and make it level. Now lay your fireplace out carefully, providing space for firebrick and keeping in mind support for the chimney, which must rest on the foundation outside of the cabin. Use your plumb line.

Do not be sparing with the mortar. Mortar must be free from gravel, not too wet. Use sifted sand mixed to a stiff paste. Place face stones about three-quarters of an inch apart; fill in between the joints. Tap the stones with the handle of a trowel until all joints are cemented well. Scrape off any surplus and throw it back into the mortar box. Mix mortar in small quantities and work it with your trowel from time to time to keep it tempered. A total of three to five shovelfuls.

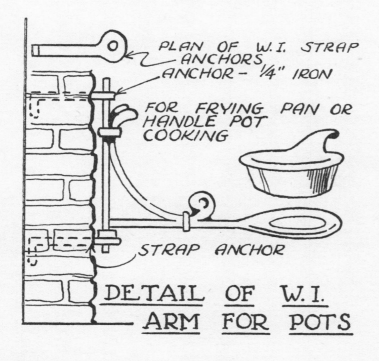

PLAN OF W.I. STRAP ANCHORS
ANCHOR - 1/4" IRON
FOR FRYING PAN OR HANDLE POT COOKING
STRAP ANCHOR

DETAIL OF W.I. ARM FOR POTS

MIXTURE

Three sand, one cement, one and one-half lime or prepared commercial mixture called brick cement—directions on the bag.

It is advisable to build the chimney of brick, enclosing the flue. Use flue lining, eight inches by twelve inches, for the fireplace with an opening of thirty-six inches by twenty-four inches. Lay the firebrick first and then build the stonework around it. This keeps the work open and easy to get at.

The inside of the raised hearth fireplace measures thirty-six inches wide, twenty to twenty-four inches in depth, and twenty-six inches high. The sides draw in slightly toward the back (about two inches each side). The back wall rises perpendicular for fourteen inches from the fireplace level, then slants upward and forward until it reaches the throat, which is at least eight inches above the arch. The throat should be at least ten percent in the square area of the opening of the fireplace. Also, the flue must be ten percent in the square area of the opening of the fireplace or better.

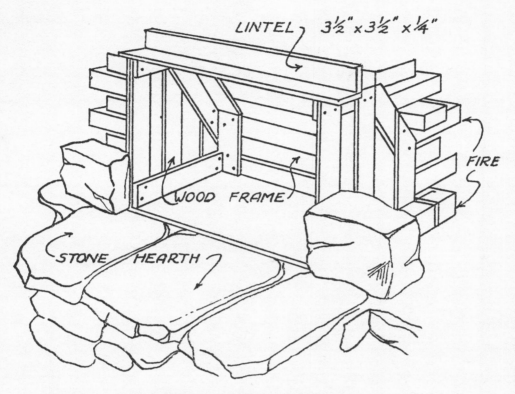

LINTEL $3\frac{1}{2}" \times 3\frac{1}{2}" \times \frac{1}{4}"$

FIRE

WOOD FRAME

STONE HEARTH

A SIMPLE METHOD FOR THE NOVICE

First, build a wooden box or frame, the outside of which will be the same as the inside space of your fireplace—throat and approach to the flue. This will save you endless trouble. Build your fireplace and mason work around the framework with reasonable certainty. Always lay brick or stone horizontally and bind one on the other. Use care in placing the damper and the two angle irons. A damper is not necessary, but will save your house from destruction by squirrels in the summer and fall; it also helps regulate draft. An old-fashioned damper such as used in woodstove pipe can be built from sheet iron and fitted in the flue just above the fireplace mantle shelf.

The rest, then, is a matter of laying one stone or brick on the other, always lapping one stone over the other, keeping all work level and perpendicular lines true.

POT HOOKS

When building your fireplace do not forget to include an iron hook on which to hang a kettle for hot water. A swinging pothook has many valuable uses—keeping food hot, keeping coffee hot, et cetera.

Ashes

IT'S time to turn in, for the hour is late. The night is still. Yet, somehow, we linger. Why? No one knows. There is always enchantment in the closing hour when the fading coals in the fire stir and "speak" their soft good night. Dying embers fall apart; the glow fades and is replaced by a delicate white ash, more beautiful than and as intriguing as the stillness of the night. Finally, we realize the great sacrament of fire is completed. A downdraft of our chimney may scatter these feathery white ashes over our hearth until one becomes entranced by the lacy white filament. "Ashes to ashes" have portrayed their fulfillment.

FIRE PLACE SCREEN

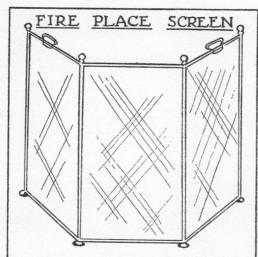

PLACE FLAT AGAINST YOUR FIRE PLACE WHEN YOU HAVE NO FIRE TO KEEP OUT FLIES AND SQUIRRELS, ETC.

FIRE PLACE TOOLS

COOKING GRATE

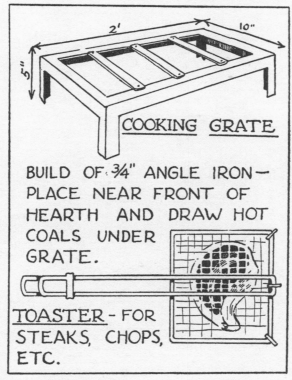

BUILD OF ¾" ANGLE IRON — PLACE NEAR FRONT OF HEARTH AND DRAW HOT COALS UNDER GRATE.

TOASTER - FOR STEAKS, CHOPS, ETC.

Somehow, I just can't bear to burn rubbish or wastepaper in a glowing fireplace. These produce a black ash. White ashes remind one of the "sacrament of fire," of God's gift, of warmth and light. The delicate loveliness of white wood ashes seems a symbol of purity and consecration. We, too, will "burn out" someday, but joyously by what we have created in our time for our own happiness and the good of the world. We, too, may contribute to life's great sacrament of fire for the generations to come.

Tricks of
the Trade

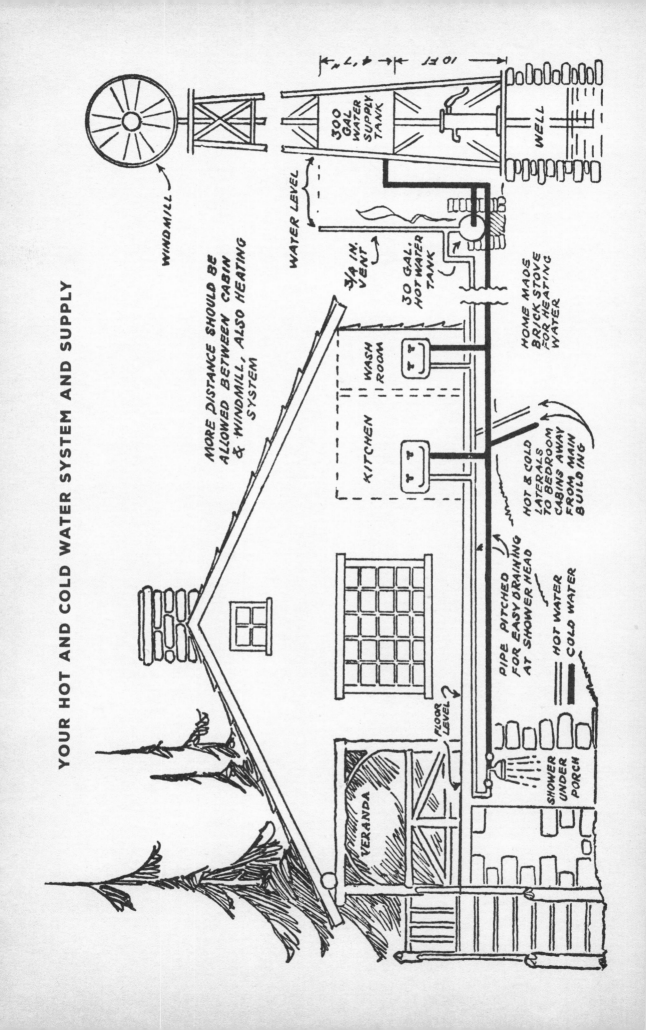

YOUR HOT AND COLD WATER SYSTEM AND SUPPLY

WINDMILL

MORE DISTANCE SHOULD BE ALLOWED BETWEEN CABIN & WINDMILL, ALSO HEATING SYSTEM

10 FT.

4' 7"

300 GAL. WATER SUPPLY TANK

WELL

WATER LEVEL

3/4 IN. VENT

30 GAL. HOT WATER TANK

HOME MADE BRICK STOVE FOR HEATING WATER

WASH ROOM

KITCHEN

HOT & COLD LATERALS TO BEDROOM CABINS AWAY FROM MAIN BUILDING

VERANDA

FLOOR LEVEL

PIPE PITCHED FOR EASY DRAINING AT SHOWER HEAD

SHOWER UNDER PORCH

HOT WATER
COLD WATER

Running Hot and Cold Water

A SUMMER camp is incomplete without a shower bath. One does not need to think in terms of tile floors or granite bathtubs. A hot and cold water system can be installed for very little cost. In fact, we built one that supplied hot and cold water to not only the shower, but also for the kitchen and washroom. It was fun to work with Stillson wrenches, valves, fittings, water pressure, air vents, et cetera.

A house-wrecking company supplied sinks, pipes, and valves at a very reasonable cost. A thirty-gallon hot water tank laid flat with a fire hole under it resulted in our hot water heating system. A wood fire built in it in the morning would smolder all day and keep water hot. On sunny days, we had a solar heating system with no effort or expense. Three oak barrels connected by pipe will store one hundred and fifty gallons of water.

Careful study of your hot and cold water system and supply tells its own story.

Waste: Johnnies
and Incinerators

TOILETS, at their best, are none too good. Most toilets in the woods smell and are a disturbance. If you insist on having a toilet inside your cabin, then you must follow certain precautions.

There are, generally speaking, three kinds of toilets—flush, septic, and old-fashioned privies.

FLUSH TOILETS

If in Your Cabin in the Woods you can have running water and proper drainage, and, if you can keep running water from freezing, install a flush toilet inside your cabin. In the far south, this may be in keeping and successful. To go to your cabin on weekends in the winter where temperatures get below freezing, you have at once a different problem. Unless you can properly shut off all water below the frost line and drain all receptacles, you will have no end of trouble and inconvenience. This, then, is a problem for your plumber.

SEPTIC SYSTEMS

Septic systems (bacteria action) can be installed inside your cabin, but you will not be pleased with the results. They give off an odor of some kind or another. On a warm still night, they exude fumes (a sweet sickly smell) that will remind you constantly of the presence of a toilet within your cabin. This kind of toilet is most successful fifty or one hundred feet or more away from your cabin. Observe local state health laws. You will, however, find them efficient and economical.

PRIVIES

The old-fashioned privy or "backhouse" is still a good type of outdoor toilet if properly built. First, the pit must be deep (five or six feet at least). Second, it must be properly boxed— and with a fly-proof seat and cover. The seat cover should be so constructed that it drops in place automatically. The building should be fly-proof and screened. This toilet should be at least fifty feet from the cabin—better, one hundred or one hundred and fifty feet away— and, by all means, away from any possible drainage toward your spring or well. Consult your local health authorities.

YOU DECIDE

It is now for you to decide where you want your toilet, according to your desires and within your means and health regulations. A "one-hole" backyard privy can be built for the cost of materials if you do the work.

Even an outdoor toilet can be built along good lines. Paint or stain it to fit into the surrounding color scheme. Plant young trees or vines to enclose it.

INCINERATORS

This subject may seem unimportant, except for the necessity of a simple daily disposal and avoidance of odors about your cabin. I have tried several kinds—wire frames, stone incinerators, et cetera. What is most needed is an efficient method of getting rid of daily waste that naturally accumulates in a cabin—wastepaper, tin cans, garbage.

I have found a plain open pit the simplest of all—a pit three feet deep by five feet in diameter. As you dig the pit, throw up a bank of dirt three feet wide all around the pit. This will raise a wall all around and will protect you against grass fires when you burn the refuse. Wrap garbage in paper, which helps in the combustion. Throw in small branches of waste wood. Build a fire in the pit and burn the refuse. If damp, spray with creosote solution, which will keep the flies away. A pit used this way will serve a year for six people. It then needs cleaning out, or dig a new pit and cover the old one.

One word of caution—place the pit so the prevailing winds will carry odors and smoke away from your cabin.

THE OIL DRUM INCINERATOR

Dig a trench eight inches deep by ten inches wide and ten feet long. Now dig another at right angles to cross the center—same length. Place an oil drum in the center, open top and with large two-inch holes punched in the bottom. You can do this with an old axe. The four trenches will carry the prevailing wind from any of four directions and travel up the oil drum. Throw wastepaper and garbage in the drum and let it burn. If garbage is balanced with paper and other inflammable material, your incinerator will smolder all day and gradually burn out. Occasionally dump the ashes, bottles, glass, and other solid material.

OTHER WASTE

Much that we throw away in the city is well worth saving in the woods—string, twine, paper from wrappings, small boxes, and cartons. You may find it more difficult to run to the store to replenish your needs. You will fully realize this, once you are "caught short."

Beautifying
Your Cabin

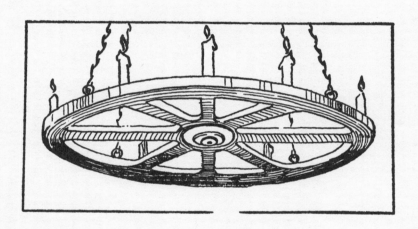

ALTHOUGH I lay no claim to knowledge of interior decoration, there are a few essentials I feel I dare suggest, which can give to the inside of your cabin home the comfortable, simple, rugged beauty in keeping with the structure and the setting.

I once saw a beautiful, truly pioneer, log cabin ruined by the successful and lovely scheme of decoration for a city home transplanted to the primitive naturalness of the country. It did not fit.

A cabin of logs suggests its own motif in both line and color. We are getting away from the artificial. We are reviving the restful softness of the woods' coloring, the strength of straight lines and natural curves, with accents of brilliance for warmth on cold nights and light on cloudy days. To achieve this rather fierce charm of ruggedness blended with coziness has a fascination all its own. Your cabin can throw a spell over one in its rough welcome, gentled by the natural refinement of your personal tastes and expressions. Even the flickering fireplace flames will enhance your cabin color scheme.

Cedar logs are tan in color with streaks of lighter tone all the way from light brown to cream. Cedar has a beautiful grain, so does hemlock when properly dressed down. Hemlock logs, however, when left to dry for a year tone down to a fine silvery gray. Cedar, thoroughly dry,

Door Latches
and shutter catches

may be dressed down with a draw-shave, reviving its natural color and releasing that sweet pungent smell of the cedar woods. Dressed knotty white pine blends perfectly with a log cabin. You can use it for doors, window frames, cupboards, and bookshelves. It does not need a dark stain. Merely rub it down with boiled linseed oil, adding a coat of varnish. The knots will glisten, the lovely natural grain remains. Without this treatment, white pine does not stay light but gets darker and darker as time goes on until it looks dark brown.

Don't miss the fun of having wrought iron hinges and latches. Plenty of imagination and personal symbolism can go into the choice of design for the door knocker to announce your visitors, the iron foot scraper, even the bootjack, that are a part of your porch decoration, and, too, door hinges and pothooks. By now you must be saying, "I have no money to spend on wrought iron." You need not say it. Go to your hardware store or, better still, to the general store in the country town. Ask for a pair of heavy barn hinges. You can get them from twenty-four to thirty inches long. Now hunt up the village blacksmith (or realize the fun of setting up a small forge of your own). Have the blacksmith reheat the metal, then pound it hard with a ball-peen hammer, roughen it, with or without design, and it becomes wrought iron. From scraps of iron and with ingenuity, many delightful articles may be added to your cabin, inside and out. Their rugged individuality suits your cabin motif. An old buggy wheel suspended from the rafters by log chains of iron may afford overhead lighting. Brackets for oil lamps add to their charm. Of course, the tools for your fireplace and the pothooks become essentials.

Speaking of indoor fireplaces, I am tempted to say here, "Don't build this center of your home, your hearth, out of manufactured bricks if natural stone is anywhere available." Native stones belong to your setting; you can't improve upon them. Use them.

Your choice of flooring may be determined by your budget—or the availability of material. Flagstone, if available. Hardwood (i.e., maple or oak) is preferable, but Georgia pine or fir, sanded, oiled, and varnished do very well.

For old times' sake, and for easy cleaning and wear, remember to include rag rugs, the kind Grandma used to make out of odds and ends of garments or old material. Here is a

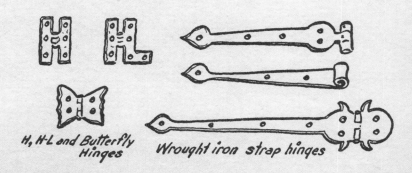

H, H-L and Butterfly Hinges   Wrought iron strap hinges

chance to learn the knack of hooking rugs. The homespun materials are in keeping with early American designs. We found burlap had that handmade look. Burlap can be purchased by the yard from your bag company. We used it for cabin drapes. It blended perfectly with the wood tones. To enliven it a bit we stenciled the borders with conventional figures in bright colors. In a cabin in the mountains, two friends of ours have created designs that express, totem pole fashion, the episodes, the fun that have grown into the life of the cabin. These designs are repeated on dishes, cushions, bookends, even hammered into some of their iron and copper work.

One other element that adds to the welcome in your cabin is, in homely phrase, a sweet, clean smell. On this point, there is need of precaution. A tightly closed, poorly ventilated cabin will soon grow musty and will disappoint you. In the gable ends, and very near the top, I have a small window swung on hinges. Attached to its top is a latchstring long enough so I may open and shut the twelve-inch opening at will. The last thing I do, when leaving my cabin, is to open the ventilators.

One other precaution you must take to preserve this fresh clean smell: If you burn wood in a stove, you must guard against the drip of creosote from the stovepipe. Wood smoke builds up creosote in your chimney flue, and in the stovepipes leading to it. When the stoves are idle, moisture gathers. Rain also may enter an uncapped chimney and carry the creosote along. It leaves a pungent and offensive odor.

I once had such a stove. The pipe ran straight up for five or six feet above the stove. Then came the elbow and two lengths of pipe that ran horizontally into the main chimney. Snow drifted into the chimney and settled in the horizontal part of the pipe. On arrival, we started our fire. The snow melted and drip, drip, drip, from the joints of the pine came the black, sticky, stinking creosote. It sputtered over the floor and even the sidewalls. Creosote is the worst stuff to scrub away, and the smell will not fade.

I have since learned I do not always need to pipe into a brick chimney. I run the stovepipe straight up and through a triple cylinder, metal smokestack right through the roof. It is perfectly safe—and cheaper than the brick. I also learned when the pipe sections are fitted one into the other it is wise to nest the top section into the one below. This does away with any possible leak of smoke or moisture. The creosote is also controlled.

WROUGHT IRON FOOT SCRAPERS

Lamps, Lighting, and Illumination

KEROSENE lamps are almost a luxury in this day of electricity. They throw long flickering shadows—so do candles. Log cabins are intimately associated with candles and kerosene lamps.

Chain-pull kerosene lamps can still be bought from secondhand stores or antique shops. I wish I could find again the beautiful hanging lamp of my boyhood days. Way back in the 1890s, as I remember, it seemed there were a "thousand" crystals hanging around the globe dome. We pulled it down over the living room table, back on the farm when the family gathered after supper and the day's work was done. A dish of apples supplied from our cellar, also a dish of hickory nuts. One of the older members of the family would crack the nuts on the bottom of the old-fashioned flatiron—the kind Mother used to heat by placing it on the top of the kitchen stove on ironing day. The real family life was around the living room table, under the dome of our chain-pull crystal-decorated lamp. Here was security—the peace and quiet companionship of the family.

The wagon wheel "chandelier" suspended from the roof-ridge with logging chains is a modern interpretation; yet it conforms to the spirit of the Cabin in the Woods. Place either lamps or candles on the rim. Here is room to follow your own fancy.

LANTERN MAGIC

What an important part the lantern has played in American pioneer life. Within the squared-oak log cabin back on the farm in Wisconsin, winter nights closed in at four or five o'clock in the afternoon. As we approached the barn to do the chores, our lantern cast great shadows of the person ahead of us on the barn wall—shadows that grew larger and larger with each approaching step, until they became giant-size. Inside the barn, the lantern was hung on a wooden peg. Each person sat on a milking stool, head pressed against the belly of a cow, pail gripped between the knees. As each pail became full, we would carry the warm milk near to the lantern, pour its contents through a clean-washed cloth strainer into the milk can, and return to the next cow for the second ten quarts. One cow I milked had the habit of switching her tail in my direction so I would place her tail between my head and the side of her belly and press hard. The smell of

129

cow dung, animal odor, the warm moisture of the barn, the smell of sweet hay, and the pungent odor of silo feed were a part of pioneer American life.

The lantern, as it cast its feeble flickering rays, was an important part of the milking ceremony. It was the only light we had.

Lanterns cast soft lights. Their "feeble" shadows teach you patience and calm. You find in them a slowing-down process. They help take you from high tension back to a wholesome normal. Try it. You, too, will discover magic in the old-fashioned lantern.

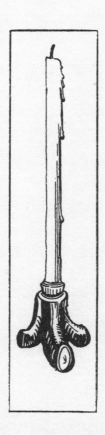

Rustic Furniture

RUSTIC furniture, inside or out, will add more than anything to the artistry and homelikeness of your camp. It is by no means difficult if built of natural rustic material because every piece of natural wood has graceful lines. However roughly fashioned, your articles will be good-looking. Rope, some bolts, a few nails, a good sharp axe, an expansion bit for boring one-inch to one-and-one-half inch holes, a draw-shave, small timber from the woods, two to four inches in diameter, and a little ingenuity are all that are needed. The illustrations may be followed exactly or make your own adaptation to suit your fancy.

A DINING ROOM SUITE

Here is an outdoor dining room outfit that costs little or nothing. On my own place, I built the table on top of a small tree stump. I cut off the stump twenty-five inches above the ground—allowing for four inches of thickness of tabletop. If you have no convenient stump, dig a hole where you want your table. Use your post-hole digger for the neat hole—about thirty inches deep. Set in it a six-inch log about five feet long. Stamp it in firmly. With your crosscut saw, level the top at the desired height.

If you have small softwood trees or saplings four to six inches in diameter, cut these in four-foot lengths and split them in half, smoothing one side flat with your axe. Next, lay these logs flat side to the ground and anchor them together with two cleats. Now place them on your post flat side up. Put four angle braces beneath.

Cover the top with linoleum and your table is ready for use.

Splitting saplings for tabletops can best be done with iron wedges. Your extra axes can serve this purpose. Start at one end of the log by driving your axe slightly, but exactly, in the center. Drive the second axe into the crack you have started—about twelve inches farther along. By the time the third axe is in place, the first axe will drop as the split log gives way. Of course, if you have lumber, you can build a tabletop with much less effort!

Peg-leg stools are a practical and natural companion to a treetop table. They are easy to make and will last a lifetime in the open. For four stools you will need two sixteen-inch-long logs about twelve inches in diameter. Split these in half, again smoothing the flat side with your axe. On the round underside bore three one-and-a-half-inch holes about three inches deep. These should be at an angle so the legs will spread. Next, cut twelve two-inch-thick

branches, three for each stool. Taper each at one end to fit snugly into the bored holes. A three-legged stool fits more easily on uneven ground than one with four legs. With the help of a friend, your complete dining room set can be built in an hour or two.

Perhaps you may have no twelve-inch softwood on your place. If not, go to your nearest telephone or electric company. For a small fee they will sell you used telephone poles. Often they have poles too short for their purposes but adequate for yours.

So, for this project you will need (1) a friend to share the fun; (2) a post-hole digger; (3) a crosscut saw; (4) an augur; (5) an axe; (6) carpentry tools; (7) wood from your woodlot. Lastly, energy and imagination if you don't want to sit on the ground.

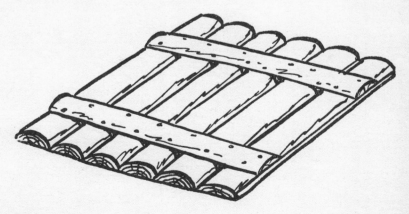

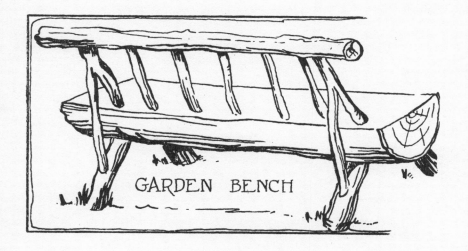

GARDEN BENCH

THE HALF-LOG BENCH

Cut six-foot logs from a fourteen- to eighteen-inch tree. Split through the middle. Bore four holes one and one-half inches at an angle in the bottom or round part of the log so the peg-legs will protrude from the seat "fore and aft" about four inches. The backrest needs one and one-half inch holes with support running to the back legs. The seat part should be dressed, planed, and sandpapered.

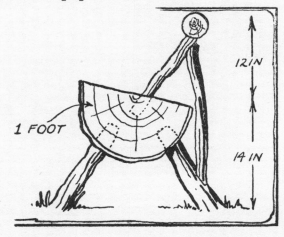

1 FOOT

12 IN

14 IN

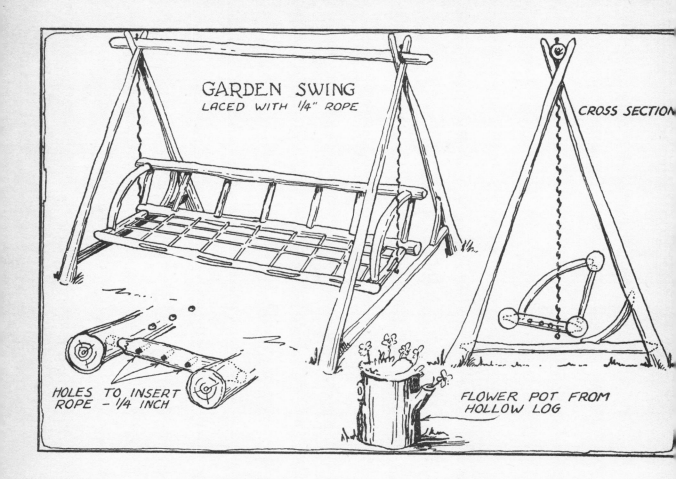

GARDEN SWING
LACED WITH 1/4" ROPE

CROSS SECTION

HOLES TO INSERT
ROPE - 1/4 INCH

FLOWER POT FROM
HOLLOW LOG

THE RUSTIC HAMMOCK
OR GARDEN SWING

Six feet six inches long, it will serve as a bed. Canvas over frame will serve as a tent and make a good extra bed when the unexpected visitor arrives. Start with the seat frame. The two end pins doweled into long ends. Then bore holes every four inches all around and lace with one-quarter-inch rope. Homemade cushions will serve for the mattress and seat. Try corn shucks for the mattress. Just fill a straw tick with handpicked corn shucks. They make a very comfortable bed. Use the soft, springy, inner part of the cornhusk. The outer leaves are harsh.

ROPE BUNKS

These make good cabin beds. Bore three-eighths-inch holes every four inches around the frame of four-inch saplings. Lace with one-quarter-inch rope. Bunks with slats on which to place springs and mattresses make good beds.

CHEST UNDER BUNKS

These serve well for storage and utility space. Casters under the chest make for easy handling.

Storm Doors

IT will help your heating problem in winter if you add storm doors to your cabin. I have seen a cabin with a picnic table with folding legs fitted as a storm door in winter, but in summer unhinged and again used as a picnic table.

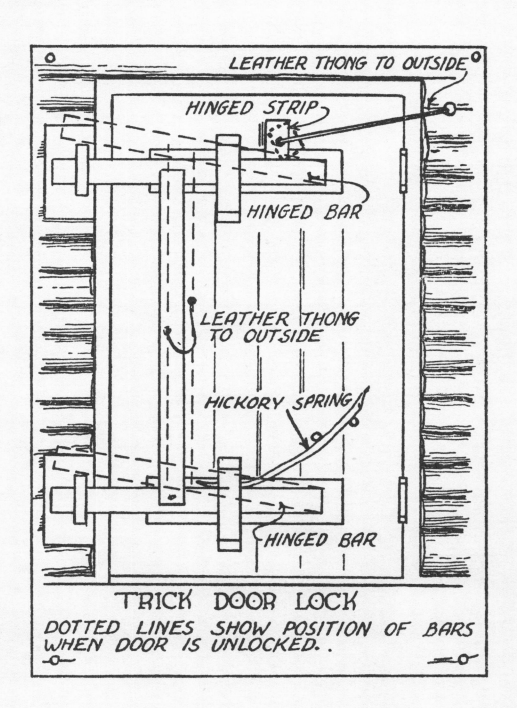

LEATHER THONG TO OUTSIDE

HINGED STRIP

HINGED BAR

LEATHER THONG
TO OUTSIDE

HICKORY SPRING

HINGED BAR

TRICK DOOR LOCK

DOTTED LINES SHOW POSITION OF BARS
WHEN DOOR IS UNLOCKED.

Trick Door with Secret Lock

WHAT could be more discouraging than to arrive at your winter cabin after a long hike, cold and a bit wet, to find you have forgotten the key? Here is a cure for that human weakness, or at least protection against it—a trick door lock. Pull a leather thong, push a slide, lift a latch, and—presto—the door opens! Work out your own combination. Make it as complicated as your imagination suggests, but don't forget the combination.

Trim Plate Decoration

A DECORATIVE effect can be given by dressing plates with half-round four-inch or split logs.

Wooden-Peg Coat Hangers

COAT hangers can be made of wooden pegs three-quarters of an inch thick. Bore three-quarter-inch holes in a log.

Skylight

A SKYLIGHT in the roof of your cabin will add light on dark days. It is also a good out for hot air.

Natural Icebox Cooler

BUILD an icebox cooler in the side of a hill. Stone walls on the sides and back. Top, dome-shaped. Use a two-inch-by-eight-inch frame with double doors inside and out. This will keep vegetables from freezing in winter, and provide cellar coolness in summer. Or build an eighteen-inch-by-eighteen-inch elevator cellar within your cabin, five feet deep. This is raised by rope and pulley. It must be supplied with outside drainage on the downside of a hill.

The Frame House

THUS far, we have discussed log cabins along very simple lines. Something now should be said for frame buildings for the person who loves the out of doors, but who prefers to erect a bit more of a modern building. Modern in the sense he prefers plastered walls inside and painted walls without. A white cottage with green blinds. Why not? I must admit I could not treat this subject with any such warmth and length as I would the lore that surrounds log cabins. Nor is it necessary. There is unlimited source material on the subject of frame buildings.

These drawings may help you. A local carpenter can be of real help. He will help you figure the amount of lumber with accuracy and without waste. Also, the length of plates, rafters, joists, windows, and board feet of lumber to complete the job. More than this, he can help you build it and with speed.

ROOF PLATES AT CORNERS

Here we have plates at the top of studding fastened at corners, also sill construction on foundation. To keep your cabin warm underfoot, it is good to build a double floor filled in between with tar paper.

The following gives construction of roof rafters and method of fastening.

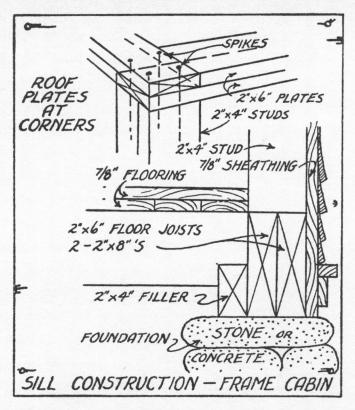

ROOF
PLATES
AT
CORNERS

SPIKES

2"x6" PLATES

2"x4" STUDS

2"x4" STUD

7/8" SHEATHING

7/8" FLOORING

2"x6" FLOOR JOISTS
2 - 2"x8"'S

2"x4" FILLER

FOUNDATION

STONE or CONCRETE

SILL CONSTRUCTION — FRAME CABIN

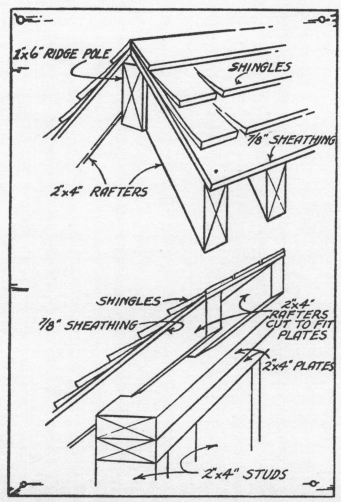

1"x6" RIDGE POLE

SHINGLES

7/8" SHEATHING

2"x4" RAFTERS

SHINGLES

7/8" SHEATHING

2"x4"
RAFTERS
CUT TO FIT
PLATES

2"x4" PLATES

2"x4" STUDS

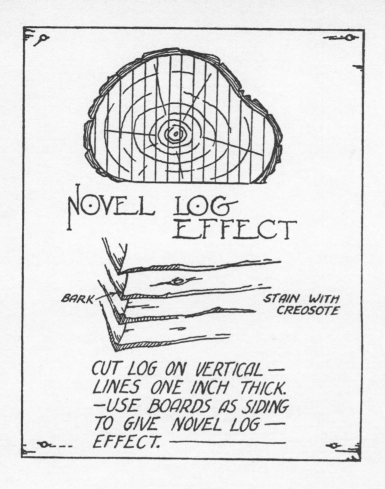

NOVEL LOG EFFECT

BARK

STAIN WITH CREOSOTE

CUT LOG ON VERTICAL — LINES ONE INCH THICK. — USE BOARDS AS SIDING TO GIVE NOVEL LOG — EFFECT. —

NOVEL LOG EFFECTS

If you want your house to look rustic you can get a clever log effect on your frame building by ripping one-inch boards off logs, going straight through the bark. After one slab is removed from the log, turn the log over to rest flat on the table of the saw. Then, one after the other, boards are ripped off. This gives you a rough edge with a strip of bark and gives you somewhat the outline of a log. Use these as clapboards with the bark end to the bottom. Cut these logs in summer or fall when there is no sap in the trees.

Flagstone Floors

IF you really want a warm, snug cabin, free from floor drafts, free from sweat, rich in design, and colorful beyond what even an inlaid floor would give, then build a flagstone floor for your cabin. Surprisingly, too, you will find the stone warmer than a wood floor.

Did you ever warm up a cabin in severe winter weather and notice the painted floor sweats great beads of moisture as the fires got under way? A flagstone floor properly laid will not do this. In fact, it will start getting warm as soon as you build a fire and it will stay warm. This is because the floor is dry and does not absorb moisture.

A flagstone floor needs, first, a foundation built all around the cabin and below frost line—four feet or better in New York State, less as you go farther south. Anchor the first log or plate to the foundation with bolts buried in the cement at least eight inches. Drainage on the outside of the cabin—that is, the ground pitches down and away from the building at least eighteen inches. Lay four to six inches of gravel within your cabin and four inches below the top of the concrete foundation. Upon this, lay your flagstone floor. After it is laid and leveled, pour a soupy, strong mixture of cement in between the flagstones. This is commonly called grouting.

If you do not have flat stones on your property, you can get pieces of marble, slate, et cetera, from a house-wrecking or construction company. Since the first log is anchored to the foundation, there is no need of binding with floor joists as in the case of a wooden floor.

Steppingstones

MANUFACTURED steppingstones may seem a bit incongruous and artificial; yet I know of places where there are no flat stones for building paths, trails, or steppingstones. I had a lot of fun once when building a cabin site in wild country where rocks were of the molten kind and I just could not get a flat surface. Then why have flat stones? Now I was determined to have them; so, having enough sand and cement, we made them. We learned some interesting things in this experiment.

First, we built pans two inches deep out of scrap sheet iron. We finally agreed on five patterns, each different so they could be fitted together in several ways. We had some red

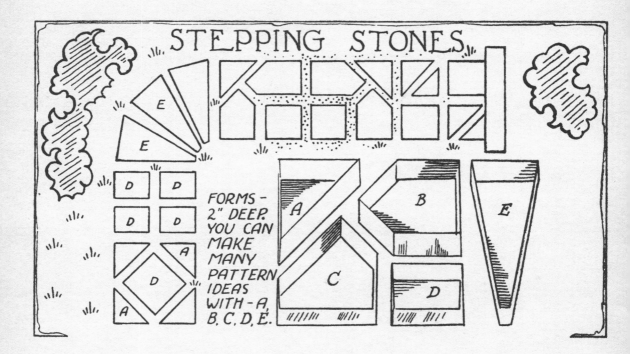

STEPPING STONES

FORMS –
2" DEEP.
YOU CAN
MAKE
MANY
PATTERN
IDEAS
WITH – A,
B, C, D, E.

sandstone chips from our fireplace, also pieces of blue and red marble. We broke these in pieces the size of hickory nuts and mixed them in the cement, and then poured the mixture into the forms. After the cement mixture "set," we smoothed the top surface with a trowel. After two days, we removed the cement blocks and rubbed them down with a common brick. To our amazement, the chips of sandstone and marble gave the cement block a really natural appearance. Still more interesting, after a month or two they weathered into soft colors that fit quite naturally into the setting.

Be sure to rub oil on the inside of your pans before pouring in the cement or you may have difficulty removing the blocks.

Personality
Plus

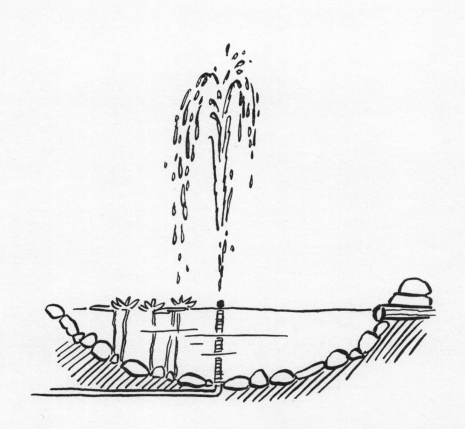

PUT personality plus into all you create. The story is told of three masons who were doing the same kind of work. A passerby inquired of each mason, "What are you doing?" "I'm laying brick," said the first mason. "I'm building a wall," the second man answered. The third mason in answer to the same question replied, "I'm building a great cathedral." Certainly, no one will question which of the three masons lived the fuller life.

And so, Mr. Cabin-Builder, I challenge you to build a "cathedral"—your greatest dream, when you create Your Cabin in the Woods. Be there woods or no, be it treeless as the Kansas prairies or the highest peaks of the Rockies— build into your cabin spot your loftiest thinking. You've got it. Think it through. It will bless you and yours if you resort not to just "laying brick or building a wall." Put personality plus into all you create.

Landscaping Your Cabin Setting

A LOG cabin needs plenty of sunlight. Logs are a fine insulation against heat, but they do absorb moisture and need to dry out. A cabin buried among too many shade trees can be dark and damp on rainy days. Leave a bit of a grass spot round the house. It really adds to the charm. One cabin builder whom I observed went to the other extreme. He decided on a two-acre lawn. With bulldozers and other machinery, he leveled his grounds—tore out wild shrubs, bushes, and small trees. He planted clover and grass. The results were beautiful but he spent much of each summer thereafter behind a lawn mower.

Bellwort

Solomon's Seal

Blue Violet

150

Salvage those small trees and bushes. Leave the natural setting, opening a vista here and there, a path or two; but let Nature, not the nursery, provide your setting. Chances are you will add a lot of extra work and expense without improving things if you go for flower beds and lawns in a big way. A Cabin in the Woods should be so simple in its setup that, after unlocking the door, opening the windows, bringing out a chair or two, you should be able to settle down and enjoy living. Breathe deep and relax.

If you want a rock garden, find it. There will be a spot somewhere that, with a few touches of recognition and encouragement, can become one. If you would like a lily pond, or even a fountain, seek your hillside spring. With a bit of piping you can guide the flow into a nearby saucer-like depression. Cover a space about ten feet wide and twelve long with cobblestones, a bit of sand and gravel. Transplant a few waterplants into the rock crevices. The fountain may be piped from below the stones. The overflow can be controlled and guided with a few clay tiles. The cost need be little. These are playthings, not work. It is satisfying to create.

Always leave something for the next visit, the next summer. Outdoor living with its relaxing, creative activity will fulfill the true purpose, the dream that went into our cabin craft.

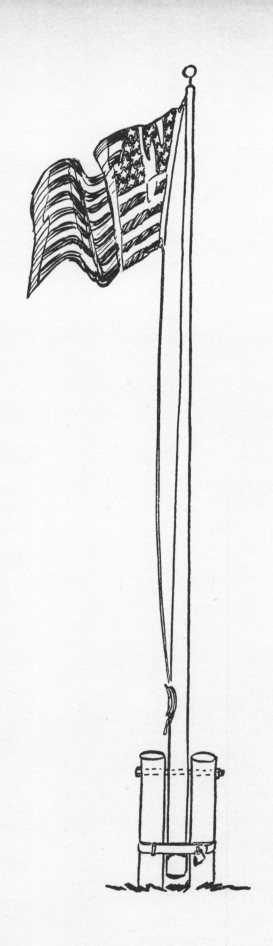

Your Flagpole

NO camp is complete without a flag and flagpole. We hoist the flag when we arrive. It says to our friends and neighbors, "We are in and you are welcome."

Were it not for the meaning woven through the years into this Flag of our Nation, we might not be enjoying the privilege of building and owning a cabin in the woods.

There are a few mechanical problems in erecting a flagpole. If you just dig a hole in the ground and drop the pole in, packing it with stones and dirt, be sure it does not lean a bit off center. This can be very distressing later! After setting, it is hard to change. So, save yourself needless hard work and disappointment. Before packing the earth around the pole be sure it stands one hundred percent perpendicular. Tie a pebble to a piece of string about two feet long. Stand about fifty feet away from the pole and hold up the string—the pebble at the bottom, of course. Here is a true vertical. Have your helpers move the pole right or left until it is in line with your plumb line. Circle the pole so you have trued it from several angles. Now brace it securely. Only when you are satisfied it is actually perpendicular, fill in around the base with dirt and stones. Tamp it in firmly. Keep it braced for a week until it settles.

I have taken for granted that before you raised the pole your pulley and halyard were in place. It is a wise man who whips the halyard lines or at least ties them together. I once had the embarrassment of having one of the lines slip out of my hand. In less time than it takes to tell it, the halyard had run out of the pulley forty feet above. Old Glory did not fly that day. It is not an easy matter to get up to the top of a graceful pole—even with a ladder. Since lines wear out or decay and have to be replaced, I now use a double post with the flag pole between—a three-quarter-inch pivot or axle running between and through the two posts and the pole—about five feet above the ground. At the bottom of the pole, place an iron band attached firmly around the two posts. Fasten with a large hasp and padlock. Your blacksmith will make this for you. By unlocking the hasp, you can now lower the pole to the ground. It can be repaired, painted, and set up again without risk to life and limb.

Use a bit of imagination in dressing up the flagpole's top. A weather vane, maybe, instead of the traditional ball. Many quaint and individual flag symbols may add to the fun and usefulness of your flagpole tradition.

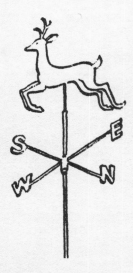

Sign Posts and Trail Markers

DOES the name you have chosen for your camp site—"Camp Elizabeth," or "Shady Pines," or, a bit flippantly, "Dew Drop Inn"—express your welcome to your friends and neighbors? Does it say, "We want you to come and share with us what we have. We delight in your coming"?

Express your personality in some sign or symbol—perhaps a pine tree cut out of metal, your name fashioned in rustic wood, a novel wrought iron lantern. Your sign or symbol will not only represent the name of your place, but the character of the people within.

Let Mother Nature Be Your Gardener

ONE of the luxuries of a Cabin in the Woods is the abundance of nearby wildflowers. Wildflowers complete the personality of gentle slopes, rugged steeps, and lush flatlands. No need of "green fingers" or a knowledge of gardening processes to have a wild garden in the country. You have the soil, sun, and moisture necessary to the flowers in your neighborhood.

If you want a more formal garden than the changing patchwork of fields beyond the windows, start with a scrap of lawn, a fieldstone terrace, or a rough fence.

To form a backdrop in our garden we have transplanted clumps of goldenrod, pepper plants from the fields, and built a loose framework of branches upon which woodbine climbs thick and green. Before it, daisies, purple bellflowers, and brown-eyed Susans are happily grouped. Down the slope in a swampy hollow are wild iris, butter-yellow cowslips, forget-me-nots, tall day lilies, and woods fern. A trickle from a spring furnishes a pool to mirror the water lilies.

Let your garden infringe upon the lawn without corners or edges or too careful trimming. Tuck tiny plants between the stones of your walk or terrace. Leave the hillocks and hollows. Accentuate them with your planting. It should look as though it just happened.

When you are strolling, watch for an unusual plant. Dig it up with care. Tie it in your kerchief to plant on your return. Try to recreate the mood of its natural setting. Space your treasure hunts throughout the summer; your garden will follow a natural sequence of bloom, for wildflowers are the hardiest of perennials.

You can let your garden grow lazily or you can become a connoisseur—searching out rare specimens. Our "showpieces" are cardinal flowers, showy lady-slippers, and a flowering dogwood. Many cultivated plants slip in among the wild ones with ease, for they are merely wildflowers with a bit of education. Hollyhocks will spread in a few years to make charming splashes of color about the garden. Golden glow, delphinium, and phlox make friends with wildflowers in bouquets, for, of course, most gardens presuppose flowers within the house.

Flower arranging may be a simple part of the morning routine. Water lilies and their pads in a shallow pottery dish make a lovely center-piece. Try a spray of goldenrod and a curve of half-ripe chokecherries over the fireplace. Pack daisies tightly in a small round bowl like an old-fashioned nosegay. Tall, orange day lilies will pay a compliment to an old bean jug.

The variety of wildflowers and their abundance are a daily challenge to expressing one's personality and mood. Even on rainy mornings, some member of the family will always enjoy bundling into a slicker and rain hat, to tramp through the tall grass and gather dripping color to make dark gray days friendly within and fresh with the woods' smell.

You may add all this variety of color to your cabin site without having to be a student of flowers. Flowers add richness and joy and interest in living. Try a wildflower garden and let Mother Nature be your gardener.

Shrubs, Trees, and Reforestation

RAISE your own forest. Plant tree seedlings and God will raise them. Plant them now. Trees are comparatively cheap as one- or two-year-old seedlings. Plant five hundred each year for ten years. You can plant five hundred seedlings with the help of another person in less than a day. Carolina poplars grow fast. They will be thirty feet high in ten years' time and give generous shade. You will revel each year in their added growth.

Plant trees native to your territory—softwood for fast growth. You can dig up quaking or bigtooth aspens most anywhere. They will grow on the poorest kind of land. Conifers can be secured from your state forestry schools—white, red, and jack pines, spruce. Would you like a ski course on your ranch? If so, plant red pines to arrest the snow on the windward side and add to your skiing and tobogganing.

Visualize the shade you will enjoy at the spot where you will have a perfect vista. Why not set out an orchard? Buy ten varieties of apple trees; include a cherry tree, crabapple, and one or two plum trees. You won't have to wait ten years for these to bear fruit. Add several nut trees—hickory, walnut, or any trees suitable to the climate you live in.

Perhaps you want a winding road to your cabin spot. Here, again, you may need trees so at each turn there may be added charm: first pines, then hemlocks, and birch. Don't fail to plant some oaks—pin oaks, red oaks, sturdy oaks. Plant them from acorns. No cost except a little effort. I planted an acorn twenty years ago just for fun. Today it is the pride of all my planting. It is now twenty-five feet high. Who knows, you may live to enjoy those plantings of your earlier days and derive peace and joy each year you live to greet them. Please, please, do not make the usual mistake of saying, "I won't live long enough to enjoy the fruits of my labors." Plant those trees this year—today—whether you are thirty, fifty, or seventy years old. They will bring you the richest returns.

Your Cabin in the Woods, if you plan with vision, will become a cabin in the woods, even though you have started on a bare hillside. Plant trees. God will do most of the work. But plant them now!

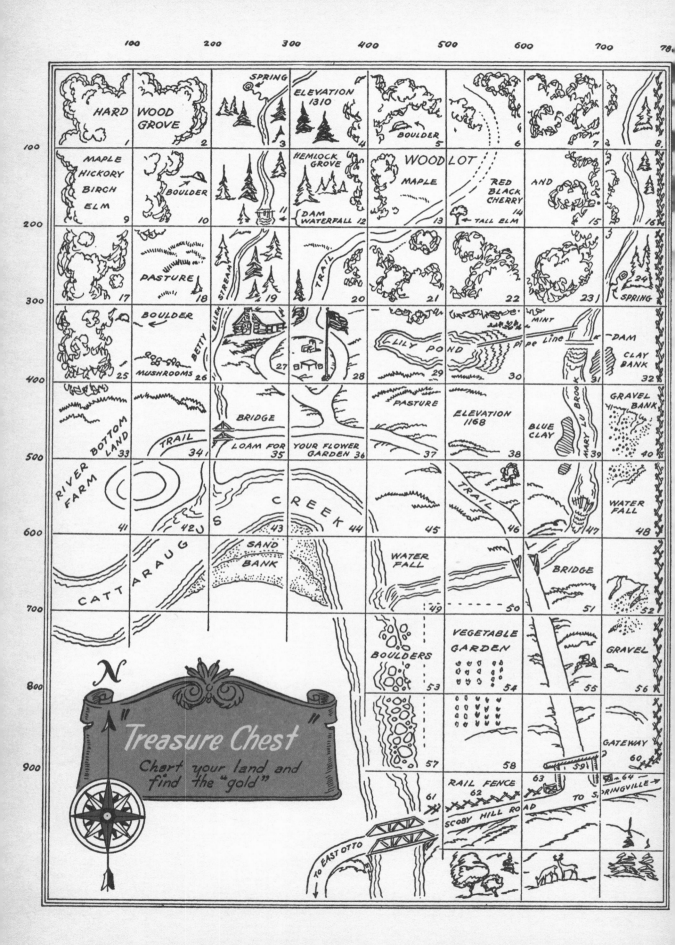

Your Treasure Chest

"THERE'S gold in them thar hills" may be said of your acres. You don't have to be a Forty-Niner, nor travel to the ends of the earth for your "gold." It is on your own land—if you know where to find it. One man turned his gravel hill into a gravel pit that paid him richly. He took toll of each load. Another discovered a clay bank. The blue gravel-free clay was suitable for fine pottery and brought a good price—and a new craft interest. A third chap made capital out of a marshy pond busy with bullfrogs. He supplies a New York market with frog's legs.

Trees planted as seedlings yield a rich return in about twenty years. Plant the type that will grow best on your particular acres. I plant five hundred evergreens each spring on my land. Now I have a hundred or more eight- and ten-foot trees that need thinning. I could sell them for Christmas trees—red pine with its long needles, balsam, white pine, spruce, hemlock, jack pine, but we will have a Christmas tree party this year for our close friends. They will come out with their kiddies and have the fun of cutting their own holiday trees.

Plant clover—red and white. It will add color to your acres and fragrance, too. Golden honey for winter sweets can be yours if you add a beehive or two, which reminds me, your maple trees will add amber syrup. This is yours for the taking—but that is another story in this book.

Rocks need not be a liability. They are wealth if used for fences, fireplaces, or other building construction. In the earth may even lie natural gas—and oil. I do not mean to be mercenary, but I do urge you to explore all the possibilities of your acres. If water is available, a sheep, a steer, or a goat that gives milk can be fed off the land—adding to your wealth with little of the routine care and housing necessary for chickens, cows, etc.

It is amazing how my little ranch blossoms and prospers each year. As soon as pine, spruce, and balsam seedlings have developed a sound root base, they seem to jump eighteen to thirty inches each year, stretching skyward a slender spire that soon branches out. Even the forgotten trees and bushes along my fences show lush growth—and behold, the highway, the passing cars become obscured. Our cabin is not only landlocked, but also tree-locked.

I'd like to share with you a device I have used to help me in the knowledge and use of resources on my land. I have made a master map. On it, I have noted the location of hickory, butternut, and black walnut trees. Here, too, are spotted a dozen old apple trees and wild thorn apple. Upon these may be grafted young apple branches that will bear fruit in a year or two. On the south hillside, just above the early frost line, I have set out a small but varied orchard—apples, plums, and cherries. Remember the luscious russets? They have almost gone out of fashion, but not in my orchard. To change a weed fruit tree into a bearing fruit of good flavor and size means careful pruning and trimming and then fertilization. I've even fussed with a thorn apple until its fruit is twice the size of its wild state. Thorn apples go back to my boyhood days, so I must have a thorn apple tree.

Let me share with you the secret for finding hidden "treasure" on your acres, the technique of mapping so you may study your land; be it one acre or a hundred, you must know it.

Test the soil value. Any county agricultural agent will help you do this and show you how to apply the treatment it needs. Study the substrata. A six-foot post-hole digger may reveal gravel or springs. Rushes, too, may indicate springs of real value. Running water means you may have fresh spring greens, watercress, and mint for your julep, and dried spices.

Study every foot of your land and you will discover hidden "gold" that will not require the miner's pick and shovel. Here's how to make the master map of your possible riches.

Let's say you have a sixteen-acre plot. This means about 800 feet by 800 feet. Start at the upper left corner. Pace off along the fence line a hundred feet. (Establish your own stride. You don't need a tape line. Mine is just two and a half feet to each step.) Plant a stake each hundred feet and repeat the process across the upper land and then down one side. You are designing an exact checkerboard picture of your land. For true reliability travel the lines down and up with a compass so your stakes—each four— will form perfect hundred-foot squares that may be represented accurately on a scale map.

Take with you a notebook and pencil. Observe and record everything you see to the left and right of your stake lines. Here—in square number ten, which would be two hundred feet east of the starting point and down one hundred and fifty feet, is a boulder of rich red stone that will be an excellent cornerstone for your cabin fireplace. Or, two hundred and fifty feet east by thirty-five feet south, is a trickling spring—or wintergreen berries—or a hickory tree for future furniture. You note that the little brook flowing down to the bottomland will assure you water for a garden regardless of the weather and could be dammed for a natural pool, or piped across lots for power, craftshop machinery, or a fountain forty feet high. (My hills run three hundred feet high.)

Now all this may sound a bit complicated. If you like what I have explained so far, let's chart this checkerboard into larger, more easily recognized zones. As you have traversed the land forward and back, you have noted landmarks more easily "picked up" than the hundred-foot stakes. Designate these on your map. This map now holds a place of honor on your cabin wall. To establish markers you may even like to erect a stone pile or cairn marker on each two-hundred-foot corner, if no outstanding landmark is nearby. This may have a name or a number on the master map. Now, when you want to relocate the hidden boulder, or the spring with its watercress, it will be an easy matter. A tall maple or a windblown elm may be your marker. You do not know one tree from another? Well, that makes it doubly interesting for now you may step into a new world—the tree world. Your five-foot bookshelf will soon harbor the best book on how to identify trees. As your respect grows, your understanding deepens, and you realize, indeed, "only God can make a tree." When this happens, you will need a

167

longer bookshelf, for you will want to know the names of the birds you see, the insects that harm and help, the history of the rock structure, the meaning of the color. You will come alive to wild plant life and wonder if these mushrooms and berries are edible. In short, the "gold" will be translated into golden light of new knowledge. You will find a new source of entertainment, of recreation. With a light heart, a grateful heart, you will find the "Golden Age of Life"—the treasure of happiness—all for the taking on your own acres. This is my idea of a paradise on earth.

So, build your master map from your field notes. Search the treetops. Search the shy wood life. Search the substrata of your land. Your map may lead you to a "buried treasure." Who knows? In this happy health-giving search, you will find more than "gold"—you will discover God in the Great Out Doors.

Sugarin'

IF your cabin is really in the woods and if you really live life in it, the urge of early spring, late February, early March will stir us to action out of doors. If further, it is located in the North Country where sugar maples grow, you'll know the sap is running. When days are

warm and sunny and nights are still frosty and clear—sap wells up from the good earth. We may tap the abundance, extract sweetness, health, and wealth from God-given nature. There never was a more delicate sugar flavor than maple syrup and maple sugar boiled down from the sap of the sugar maple tree.

A healthy tree, in a normal sap season, produces twenty-four to thirty gallons of sap. Boiled down, this will produce nearly a gallon of rich maple syrup. Have you one tree, or a grove of them? With a bit of effort, you can "sugar off." Just an iron kettle on the kitchen stove will do.

Bore a three-eighths-inch hole in the tree about three feet from the ground. Bore it about two inches deep, pointing your brace and bit straight in. Next drive in tightly a spout or spile, which can be purchased at the hardware store. Now, hang upon the spout a small pail and, at once, you will see almost a miracle. Here is the proverbial "milk and honey" right in your own backyard. As the bucket fills, carry it inside to the iron kettle. Set it to boil as you would the teakettle. As it boils down add more sap. Before too long the liquid will take on a bright, light amber color. First-run syrup of the

highest grade is judged on its weight and color. The browner syrup color seems to depend on the seasonal variation. To test for the right consistency, instruments have been invented to measure specific gravity. Do not let this disturb you. Our grandfathers had a simpler method that worked. They used just plain "horse sense." When the syrup begins to thicken, put a drop of it between your thumb and first finger. Feel for stickiness. It should feel like light mucilage. Another test is to lift a spoonful of syrup and watch it flow. If it flows like water, boil it some more. If it flows like a salad oil or light honey, it is ready for bottling. Seal it in sterile jars. You will look with pride in the months ahead on this stored-up life-giving energy, which can serve to dress up many a meal. Hot biscuits, fried cornmeal, hot cereals, French toast, ice cream, puddings, and all manner of pancakes, waffles, and fritters are enhanced with this sweetest of sweets.

Some of my happiest boyhood recollections go back to "sugarin'." We had a thousand or more maple trees. This required a sugarhouse with a sap pan, four feet by ten and about five inches deep. The pan was built or set upon brick walls that served to hold the wood fire. A chimney rose from the end farthest from the door. Our sugarhouse was made of logs, unchinked, to allow the steam from the boiling to make its escape. A cupola top directly over the pans was open on all sides to allow for additional steam escape. It was located on the side of a hill so the stone boat with its four-hundred-gallon barrel for gathering sap was able to deliver its load to the storage tank below the road but above the level of the boiling vats. No one had to carry sap uphill.

My buddy, Nicki, and I hitchhiked on the tail end of the stone boat while two hired men, one on either side of the tank, trotted to the trees for the full sap buckets, replaced them with empty ones, running back and forth to the slow-moving stone boat to empty their loads. The years of logging and sugaring had worn rude trails through the trees. In a year of abundant flow, one thousand buckets had to be emptied each day of the run. It was Uncle Claude's job to keep up the fires to keep the vats and pans boiling, boiling, boiling. The steam was so thick one couldn't see the length of the sugarhouse. These were no eight-hour days. We stayed with the job as long as the sap ran. It was satisfying. We felt rich and prosperous, with little concern about tomorrow. The good earth was giving generously. This fine flow meant profits as well as added home comforts.

When darkness fell and the last trip through the trees was hauled in, the real fun of sugarin' began. Usually we were early-to-bed folks, but, at sap time, the lid was off. Neighbors drifted in and out to taste and chat. As the syrup began to form in the syrup pan, it was ladled off just for fun. We dripped it over a pan of clean packed snow. It congealed in sticky strands that could be wound on smooth sticks or forks and munched like soft taffy. Each winter we revive the thrilling memories with sugar on snow—made in a kitchen. When the mood suited, or when Ken thought to bring his mouth organ, there was singing—such harmony—such barbershop minors—such spirit. Sometimes it was a planned party with home-made bread, and ham roasted in the coals. The sharp, salty flavor was a nice contrast to the rich sweetness. There were eggs hardboiled in the sap. Broiled bits of salt pork and bacon.

When the happy crowd recalled the program of their own tomorrows, they left us. The menfolk, who must stay 'til the syrup was run into the new shiny cans, settled down to a card game. The cards were extracted from between two logs. They stuck together a bit, but we didn't mind. It was all part of the game.

So when February comes along, let's make syrup. If you haven't a maple tree, look for the mists rising over the maple groves in the nearby country. Any farmer will enjoy sharing the fun of his sugarin' with you. Just as the golden syrup is yours for the taking, so is the friendliness of shared experience. We can still use today these solid friendly values.

"Tune In" on the Birds

BIRDS will come to your cabin and sing for you, if you encourage them. Feed and house them and their songs will gladden your heart. If you are unfamiliar with bird life, you will soon discover a new interest and hobby. But more than this, Your Cabin in the Woods will become enchanted—a rendezvous for birds.

Build a rustic, simple feeding station. Build a box of half-inch wire mesh, fill it with suet occasionally, and then watch the fun.

Besides giving us abounding pleasure in song and color, birds have a real economic value, and your interest in and conservation of bird life is important. Birds protect vegetation, which is so necessary for man's very existence. Some birds "police" the grounds, some the tree trunks, others the branches and leaves, and still others the air—all devouring the destructive grubs and insects that would despoil our vegetation. Without vegetation, our streams would dry up; without our water supply, the human race would not exist. A small effort on your part to attract the birds will be a contribution toward all humankind.

Before winter is over, try to erect birdhouses for bluebirds, wrens, and martins. Plant, if you can, thick clumps of bushes for catbirds and chirping sparrows, a trumpet vine for the hummingbird, and a mulberry tree for the later joy of midsummer birds.

The spring migration starts in late February and lasts until June. It is a thrilling experience to keep count of the different kinds of birds that visit you. A good bird reference book and a pair of field glasses will help you identify your visitors from other climates and other lands.

In the fall, put out feeding stations. While our wintering birds are relatively few, the chickadee, the downy and hairy woodpeckers, and the nuthatches will come to feast near your windows throughout the winter months. For the effort made to attract and befriend the birds that come to your locality, I know of no other reward so gratifying. If you must have a pet housecat, provide her with a collar and small bell, so the birds will have a fair chance to save themselves when the cat is abroad. This simple remedy to bird destruction is one big step toward success in being the good neighbor to your birds. The soft tinkle of the bell will alarm the birds no matter how carefully puss creeps up on them.

Birds will bring music to your cabin.

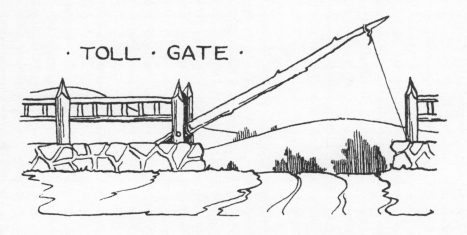

· TOLL · GATE ·

Gateways, Guardrails, Fences, and Friendliness

AS we pass through the gateway of our camp once the gate is closed, we are alone within. A closed gate implies privacy and the stranger will not intrude incautiously. However, too many people look upon a gate as a means of shutting out. Let us remember the old gate swings in as well as out, bidding you welcome and inviting you to come again.

As far as history records, gateways depicted the personality of peoples and much of the art of the age. In the Roman days when warriors returned from triumphant battles, they were formally met by the governor or high priest at the gateway of the city and, here, welcomed and honored. In ancient times, great cities were enclosed with high stone walls. Pretentious gateways were provided for the inhabitants to come and go on their peaceful pursuits. On

PIONEER

GARRISON

CHINOOK

ALAMO

state occasions, the gateway to a city was the
formal meeting place—the place for salutations;
the crossing of swords. Lords and ladies were
dressed in their finest—deep curtsies, sly flirt-
ations, clicking of heels, salutes. In a word, the
town was celebrating and came to its gateway
to welcome honored guests and heroes.

In more modern days, gateways still hold
an important part in our communal life. What
a thrill on arriving in one of our great cities to
step off a train and into a beautiful, yes, by its
very bigness, inspiring railway station. This is
a modern city's gateway for its friends and
inhabitants.

Now we are inside your gateway and following
a winding road with changing vistas at each
turn. The bank is steep on one side so a
guardrail is on the curve to guide our guests
who may walk or drive in the night—white-
washed boulders or perhaps a sign or symbol
to give them direction.

As you enter the cabin door, the mat may have the word "WELCOME" woven into it. Often wrought iron lamps on either side of the door light your way and add welcome.

Your spot in the woods, however large or small, should be enclosed with a fence—a fence that expresses the artistry and, indeed, the personality of the owner. As for myself, I would choose the old rail fence because of my childhood memories. In my boyhood days, we held basket picnics next to the rail fence and the big elm tree. Those were sweet experiences. The spot was a sort of playground for neighborhood folks both young and old. We'd meet at the big elm next to the rail fence. And, so, rail fences warm me. They belong to my youth. They belong to me now. After all, rail fences are just as good as any other kind of fence if you can get them. They are simple to build. They have a sturdy, homely dignity. I must admit I bought nearly three-quarters of a mile of rail fence from a farmer one time. He was tearing his fence down. I bought it out of sentiment more than actual need. I'm sure he must have said under his breath, "They ain't worth cuttin' up for firewood."

WESTERN

SWANEE

YANKEE

Friendly Trails

TRAILS are plain paths or obscure wind-ings among trees, rocks, or boulders.. They become more pronounced by use. Obscure trails are more intriguing. Step over a log or rock. Make your trail interesting, especially if it leads to your favorite hiding spot where you may want to be alone—away from the world. Or it may lead to your bird sanctuary or to a pet chipmunk who will come to you if you call and will eat from your hand.

You may want your trail to lead to a one-man shack, tucked away out of view. Put a small fireplace in the shack, a bunk, a book or two. Build it out of natural resources. Don't spend too much money. Go to it some starlit night. Take a friend in tune with your thinking. Here you will find the romance of "night, God, and the Milky Way."

This may sound like a three-hundred-acre tract. No, I'm thinking of one, two, or ten acres. Of course, if you are lucky enough to have more land, so much the better. Do you still have a farm belonging to the family from your childhood days? Don't let it get out of the family. Divide it, if need be, but hold on to it. Some day when you reach the age of forty, you will wish you still had it, for just such a purpose as we are discussing. It has too many rich treasures and traditions to let it out of family hands. You will, at some time in later years, "revert back to the land."

To get back to trails, remember trails are undeveloped paths, not too obvious, not too clear cut. Leave something to the imagination.

"Shall we turn right or left? Now let's see . . . there are three stone markers, first a large one, then a smaller one, and a still smaller one taking the shape of the point of an arrow." This is stalking.

Go alone. Sit by yourself and suddenly with God. If you have never done it, you will have a new experience. Birds will fly overhead. A chipmunk may chatter, a katydid may say its say, and you will suddenly find yourself with God and at peace with the world. This is Christ in the mountains. You will find this a place for clear thinking on the eternal fitness of things.

So, my friend, your trail has not only led you to a place, but to a new opportunity—perhaps a challenge. Perhaps you will have really discovered yourself.

Springs

PURE drinking water is as essential as pure air. There is something about spring water that is different from any other form of drinking water. It is refreshingly cool and, yet, though one drinks great drafts of it, it is not like ice water in its effect upon one's stomach.

I have a favorite spring to which I trudge a mile just for a deep satisfying drink. The spring forms a deep pool surrounded by moss and rocks. Watercress and fresh greens line the sides of the little stream below. Somehow, I grow sentimental and make a ceremony of the approach. To lie flat on one's stomach is not at all undignified— prone, nestling close to Mother Earth—lips touching the sparkling water. I cannot stop there. Face deeper and deeper into the spring, until opening my immersed eyes I behold a new world. The crystal water serves as a magnifying glass, showing the delicate plant life, the bubbling particles of white sand dancing playfully about those small apertures in the earth from which flows this frolicking stream. Then up again for a breath of God's fresh air. And again and again a deep draft. Why must I return to the kitchen faucet to draw a glass of chlorinated, medicated fluid that is hopefully labeled "pure drinking water"?

Indian Cucumber

WILD MINT

Life in the outdoors may take the crease out of one's trousers, but it will leave impressions of things fundamental, values against which to judge the shallowness of modern civilization. A great crony of mine, Samuel Bogan, once invited me to his "hermit's shack" in Connecticut for a weekend. He waxed warm about his favorite spring, which was nearby. We both went to visit it, to drink deeply from its cool waters. As we sat there, he told me of its history. I said, "Sam, write what you have just told me." He did and here it is—a classic legend of an ageless spring in the woods:

> *I suppose most of us are amphibians at heart. We like to rest beside a flowing stream. We feel, with Seneca, that "where the spring rises and the river flows, there we should build our altars and offer our sacrifices." We like rain, and clear lakes, and mountain brooks that sing. We like water done up in glaciers, and the magnificent undrinkable sea.*
>
> *When my own spirit is battered and I am possessed of that indefinable thirst not quenched by ordinary water, I like to go to my favorite spring. It lies in the forest at the foot of a long sweeping hill, and the water comes from deep rock crevices. It is a pure spring and its flow does not change with the seasons. Its temperature is the same the whole year round. The pressure of the great hill pushes the water outward,*

and the pressure of the water throws up a small fountain of sand. The little grains of clear and milky quartz form a cascade at the bottom of the transparent basin.

The water is clear, but the spring is not colorless. The adjacent earth and sky hide nothing from it. The sky rests there and the trees are reflected upside-down. It is as though one could reach into the spring and touch the sky, or wrap one's finger in a cloud, or pluck a leaf from the tiny trees. Then, suddenly, like Narcissus, you see your face. Yet, if you look closely at your face in the spring, it shuts out the sky. It is a reminder that "he who loves himself will have no rivals."

The spring, walled in by moss-covered rocks, is as old and as permanent as the contours of the land in which it lies.

It was formed when the last glacier receded from New England some thirty thousand years ago. This is to realize, with awe, that prehistoric animals have drunk from it.

Once, in cleaning it out, we found an arrowhead. What brave left it, and in what year? The pioneers came, too. They lived near, and planted apples and maples. Where did they go and why? Westward, with the Forty-Niners? To the prairies? The wide Pacific?

Yesterday, that is to say, only fifty years ago, a hermit built a cabin on the slope and the spring was his for a while and takes its name from him, Hermit's Spring.

Curled Dock

The spring is indescribable because, being perfect, it is not supposed to exist. Have we not heard, many times, nothing is perfect? But I know better. I have seen the leaves of autumn on this spring, and the pebble-tossing fountain on its floor. I have seen within it the blue inverted sky, and a flight of birds across the sky. I knew the leaves were perfect, and the fountain, and the sky, but once, when on a clear winter night, I drank from it and suddenly realized my face was immersed in a cool sky of stars, and my spirit rested for a while. I was not thirsty anymore.

God has provided us with refreshment for our souls, with fresh air and good water, but somehow we are careless in our use and care of them. If you have a spring on your acres, be sure to protect it against contamination. If it is on a hillside, build a ditch above it so seepage water will be turned aside and there will be no possible pollution. I have added to the ditch a protecting fence to keep out wandering animals, a neighbor's cow, or thoughtless visitors unfamiliar with the ways of the woods and the value of natural resources.

chickory

Your Family
Camp on
Wheels

A SSUMING you have an automobile, assuming you are an unlucky devil who gets but two weeks' vacation— let's put it in reverse. A two-week vacation with pay implies you have a steady job, that you are a lucky devil with a job and a two-week vacation with pay. You want to make that vacation a delight and real adventure for your growing family. If you use your wits, your initiative, and resourcefulness, you can make these two weeks rich, sparkling, and satisfying even if your wage is not large. Work should give us something more than just bread. With skillful planning, the zest, the fun, the shared growing experiences of a year's hard work can be climaxed with a larking adventure together, if you would like it, in a gypsy wagon or a Family Camp on Wheels.

A Family Camp on Wheels can be yours for almost a song. Your campsite may be anywhere in North America—or points beyond. In the United States, we may travel from state to state without having to show visa or passport. Innumerable camping grounds are open to the public. Many woodland spots, offering more privacy, are also available to the careful camper. I like to think of Wisconsin with its myriad large and small lakes as the camping playground of America. Then, too, the hundreds of national parks, from the friendly Adirondack peaks to

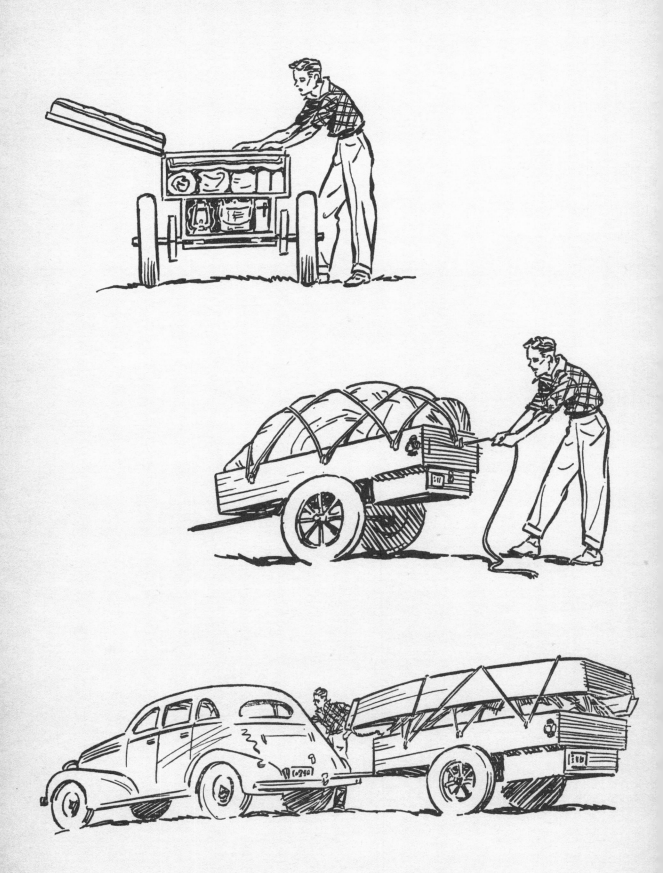

the staggering grandeur of the Rockies, from Maine to Mexico, offer us all their beauty. Your vacation need not be confined to summer months. "June may be had by the poorest comer," for this country is so large and vast one may find June weather every month of the year.

Over the past twenty-five years, we have owned the trailer from which these illustrations have been drawn. I have taken my family with me far and wide. First came the heated debate, "Where shall we go?" There was no need to make resort reservations months in advance. We did study geography, interesting places, road maps. The timetable need not depend on railroads, conducted tourist schedules, nor taxis. Our course was tempered to the time allowed—a month, two weeks, a weekend, and the size of our pocketbook. It didn't cost much more to feed the family en route than it did at home. There was only one thing to do. We packed our little covered wagon, checking and rechecking lists of food and fixings for comfort, fun, fellowship. We hitched it behind our car. Ready for the road, we were off to a new adventure.

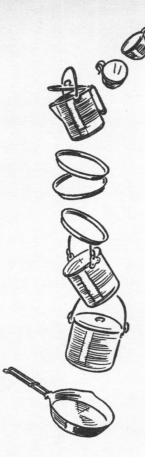

Believe it or not, my Family Camp on Wheels has spring beds and good mattresses for four persons—yes, even six with a bit more careful packing and an added small tent. It carries complete kitchen gear—pots, pans, and dishes, stove, icebox, tools for repairs, portable toilet. Not only these, but a collapsible table with a roll-up top and folding chairs and stools. We have, also, a real shower bath, with adequate privacy. Soap and water are far too cheap for campers to tolerate unclean bodies.

Part of our equipment was a shovel, rake, broom, and pickaxe—all small. We must keep compactness in mind. While we started out with pie tins for plates, tin cups, etc., we finally improved our kitchen and saved space with nesting aluminum. Four pots nested into one another—containing four soup bowls, cups, knives, forks, and spoons. This group rested on four plates nested into two skillets. The entire unit fit into a waterproof canvas bag and took less space than a water pail. Our stove and

reflector oven collapsed into a flat package. With four pairs of busy hands, the whole camp could be set up in less than thirty minutes. We made a game of it—improving our setting-up record as you would improve your golf score.

Of course, packing four persons into this little "hotel" was a bit intimate, but usually it was a family circle. Let's not forget our living "room," and play "room," and (on pleasant days), our dining "room" were the whole outdoors. Even on rainy days when our table was set back under the small canvas porch, and we were dressed in boots, raincoats, and hats, there was room to stretch and play beyond and around our tent.

Where shall we go this time? That all-adventurous question! Suppose it were a lovely weekend in early fall or spring, when an extra Saturday or Monday was available. We'd have studied the county geodetic maps, which revealed the contour lines and pointed out rugged rolling country with large and small streams. We'd trail

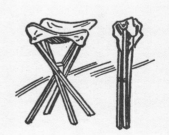

along the concrete highway and then choose an intriguing dirt crossroad that our map had shown led to some such wild spot. Farmers who have settled in these solitudes are usually friendly folk who enjoy the surprise of a contact with the outside world. "Sure, you can camp in our orchard. Drive right down the lane. Anything you want?" I have always preferred to pay for this privilege. Most often a dollar would be ample. The farmer, too, would gladly sell us vegetables and eggs, and his wife a loaf of homemade bread. You are pretty sure, too, to have a return invitation if you have been a good and tidy camper.

So we'd drive in, choose the apple orchard if there was one, strip the waterproof canvas cover from the trailer top, open out the double bed-springs, erect the canvas tent over them, anchor the fly. The stove would be set up in a safe spot, handy to the dining "room" of the moment, yet where the wind would not carry the smoke into the trailer. Soon a bright fire would do its work and savory odors would whet the appetites of the rest of the workers, who were setting up the shower bath. It was a simple contraption, this shower bath. A five-gallon collapsible canvas bucket into the bottom of which had been set a spigot. (You can secure this at any hardware store—the kind to which you can attach a bathroom hose and sprinkler.) A rope was tied

to the bucket handle. The other end of the rope was slung over the branch of a tree about seven feet from the ground. A strip of canvas, six feet high and about ten feet long, could be strung around the bucket for privacy. A small box for a stool, soap, and towel; the bucket filled from the pail now steaming gently over the fire and, "your bath is ready." This is the life, and no large fee for room and bath.

Of course, I haven't mentioned in my preoccupation with this refreshing finale before dinner that the bedding had been tucked in over the mattresses (always held in place for traveling by straps). That the icebox had been snuggled into a shady hole, and the toilet set out of sight; the lanterns filled and hung to thwart the twilight, and the tabletop set onto its frame and centered with leaves, blossoms, and berries.

One year, I had the rare privilege of a two-month vacation. We decided to go south. We took our two daughters out of school for February and March and traveled from our home in New York State to Florida and back. The school principal agreed with us that the youngsters could learn more of geography, history, life, and people than in a year of school days.

We decided the fun should begin from the moment we left home behind us. So often it is possible to spoil the present by rushing to a given

destination, with no sense of leisurely discovering the fun and knowledge to be had along the way. The person at the wheel is so often to blame for this rushing and fast driving. Why will some people have such perverse notions! I'm really talking about myself and some things I had to learn to provide riding comfort and true enjoyment. I finally got over trying to pack a month's travel into two weeks. A little paper and pencil work was needed. Three thousand miles packed into ten days would require seven hours of steady driving with an average of forty miles per hour. This would mean holding close to fifty miles per hour to maintain a forty-mile average. If you want to make a long, rush trip, then you won't enjoy your covered wagon or trailer. I learned, too, the Family Camp on Wheels is best at thirty-five mile per hour, which provides opportunity for all to enjoy the countryside, historical markers, and an occasional stop for points of interest. Someone in the car remarks there is a signpost ahead, looks like the marker of a historic spot, but Father, having gotten his car to that fifty-five- or sixty-mile tempo of speed, swishes by and then says apologetically, "Well, that's too bad. I couldn't slow up in time." Then he resumes his same safe and sane driving— fifty, fifty-five, sixty. Along at three o'clock in the afternoon Mother remarks casually, "Let's

stop at the next farm where there is a vegetable stand." Soon we come to one, but, again, Father, who seems by now to have but one focus point, the destination three thousand miles away, drives on. The family yells in unison, "Here are vegetables!" but, alas, Father, with foot deep on the gas pedal, swishes by again—and again says he is sorry. We then drive the next hundred miles with no vegetables offered for sale. True, we made another added hundred miles today. It's now near seven o'clock. Kiddies, weary and hungry, and Mother—well it just isn't fun. We compromise by eating at a "dog" stand, find a place to set up our camp—anyplace, anywhere—just so we can go to bed. We are weary. So (reward for his pressure driving), the family remains in the car as the chill of the night comes. Father sets up his clever little Family Camp on Wheels by himself in the dark. Where did I leave the flashlight?

A Family Camp on Wheels should mean more than a place to sleep. It's what the name implies and, so, I recommend this kind of trailer for longer encampments and shorter hauls. I have learned, too, for mental happiness and maximum of camping fun: stop driving at three in the afternoon and set up camp. Take time to set up properly near a brook or stream. Enjoy the fun of preparing an outdoor meal. Indeed, the place of your choosing may be so ideal you may decide to spend a few days. Why not be sufficiently mentally carefree to react to this kind of adjustment?

After many trailer trips, we actually added a small rowboat or dinghy, nine feet long, three and a half feet at the beam, a small outboard motor, and a surfboard. No, I'm not bragging. The surfboard was rigged from an old woodshed door, but it worked wonderfully. The board, motor, and surfboard idea came about when we had the two months in Florida. We envisioned ourselves within the sound of the ocean surf on a sandy beach. We dreamed of the early morning dip in the ocean, but no such luck. Choice sandy beach spots were privately owned and public beaches were controlled by local "city fathers." Those with trailers were politely told of the city block set aside for trailer campers and the law forbade any other camp spots. The city lot for trailer campers is well set up—usually electric lights with central shower baths and washrooms and other accommodations, but more congested than our closely populated city homes. We did find seclusion by renting a two-acre orange grove for almost a song ($15 per month)—just two miles from the ocean. And so we had the privacy we wanted and yet all the ocean bathing and surfboat riding. No one aboard the swanky launches, nor atop the curved commercial surfboards, learned more of balance and grace, or had more fun in and out of the waves than did my small daughters. It was satisfying to see them swaying, winging, or diving into the wake, swimming strongly until I came around to take them aboard. I was more than content to operate the boat and laugh.

You may now decide, "This man is talking about a thousand-dollar venture." Not so fast. I'm a poor man like most people and I wouldn't trade with any man of wealth whose only skill is to make money and buy luxuries. Would two hundred dollars for the outfit I have described seem an orgy of wild spending to get started? All right then. Let me set out the costs in a bit more detail.

The trailer of the illustration is a commercial product of early vintage. A friend of mine built his own using mine for a model. Through his mechanic he secured axles, three wheels (the third a spare), and springs. He built a box for it, four feet by seven by one foot deep. Attached to each side was a bedspring four feet wide. These were hinged so they could fold over the box, one upon the other. To each he

strapped a mattress. Under the floor of the box he built a cupboard to hold gear and equipment. The canvas tent, which folded into the box, was an odd shape—twelve feet wide, seven feet deep, and seven feet from trailer floor to the peak. Attached to the front was a canvas porch twelve feet wide and seven feet deep. Being handy with tools, he bought the canvas and other material for the inner frame and fashioned his trailer camp during the winter months in his workshop. Sometimes I think the anticipation is as great as the realization. They certainly go hand in hand. The family share in the planning and in the work. He even rebuilt an old outboard motor, watched for bargains in boats that were sound but needful of paint and patching. His living equipment, like ours, has grown through the years. I am proud of him. Our families spent the next summer vacationing together. He and I sat proudly watching our happy offspring who were finding the fun of God's Great Out Doors— enjoying the fruits of our winter workshop labors. "Well," Bill said to me, "You get out of it just what you put in—yes, with real interest."

"If you didn't have it—this Family Camp on Wheels, what kind of a camp would you most like to have?"

He gave me that classic answer, "I'd have a Family Camp on Wheels." And so would I!

During these twenty-five years with our Family Camp on Wheels, we have camped on many lovely camping spots—beside brooks, streams, lakes. Often the family would say after a long weekend in the woods, "Can we buy a place like this?" Well the "miracle" happened—and all within our pocketbook. You, too, can find your dream spot—land for one, five, or ten dollars per acre. If too barren, plant trees. They will grow with your love of the place.

We found our spot in the great Zoar Valley near Springville, New York. It is bounded by the onrushing, swirling Cattaraugus on one side. On the other, encircling woodland hills extend to the skies. It is far too rough for pasture, and with just a bit of river-bottom land for gardening. Three babbling brooks slosh and tumble down the wooded slopes. Hemlock aplenty for real log cabins someday. There are wild grapes and berries for the taking. Frogs and frog's legs for dinner. Mint for juleps. Wild roots for salads. Springs for cool drinks. Hickory and walnut trees for nuts and their winter fun. Crabapple and apple trees planted by pioneers of an earlier generation. Here we will trim, graft new life, spray, and have perfect apples again.

We have stopped being roamers. We have taken our beloved Family Camp on Wheels off the highway, recalling the days when it said to us, "Come on. Let's go! I just can't stay folded up," and we didn't talk back, we just packed up and went—to Maine, to Quebec, to Wisconsin, to Carolina.

But we have taken the trailer off the highway. Like the old fire horse, we turned it out to pasture. It now serves as the guest camp on our own little ranch and seems content. Soon we shall build a small cabin. We will build it ourselves, as we built up our trailer equipment.

You, too, may have your Family Camp on Wheels, or Your Cabin in the Woods, if such as these are your dreams.

Outdoor Fires
and Cooking

THIS simple outdoor fireplace is easily constructed if you have stones. You do not need plaster or cement. It can be laid up just as a stone wall is laid. If you have clay on your land, it will serve perfectly as a binder. The cost involved will be for a grate. With this type of open fireplace, it is best to let your firewood burn until you have a thick bed of coals before placing your cooking utensils on the grate. This will avoid a lot of pot-black on your kettles from the smoke.

The outdoor fireplace with the chimney is really the best for all-round efficiency. Build the chimney at least six feet high. It will carry the smoke above your head, especially if the wind is contrary. Standing in front of an open fire, your body somehow acts as a chimney wall and the smoke will travel toward you and of course, get into your eyes and lungs. So the chimney on your outdoor fireplace is worth the time and effort it takes to build it.

Chimney construction in an outdoor fireplace is indeed simple. It does not call for any of the rules required in building a fireplace in your cabin. An inside fireplace is more or less draft controlled. It burns best when all doors and windows are closed. There is usually enough seepage of air from cabin windows and doors to supply a slight flow of air to the fireplace. Opening a window just a half-inch will help the circulation and air-flow. Then, too, the inside fireplace must be correctly built; i.e., smoke shelf just inside and below the flue; also smoke pockets. There is an exact relationship of the throat to the opening of your fireplace.

In the outdoor fireplace, you need not be concerned with these building pre-

cautions. All you need is the fire pit and a flue large enough to carry off the smoke.

The grate covering your ash pit should be eighteen inches wide by twenty-four inches deep. The front of the chimney should start at the far end of the grate. In my own outdoor fireplace, I have added a three-sixteenths-inch steel plate, eighteen by twenty-four inches. Here we have the same as the top of a kitchen stove without the pot holes. With this steel plate cover, the draft travels in from the front through the fire pit and up the chimney. The steel plate has the added value of keeping your kettles free from smoke. It will give ample heat for all cooking except broiling steaks. To broil steaks or chops, remove the steel plate, and your bed of hot coals under the grate should be perfect to roast your meat—rare, medium, or well done.

At this point, the coals in the fire pit no longer need any draft. Instead of building a damper within your chimney, a simple device will do just as well, and, again, without cost.

Just a piece of tin or sheet iron placed on top of the chimney flue will immediately shut off all draft. If there is still smoke from bits of burning wood just slide the tin damper a bit to one side to allow the smoke to escape.

If there is danger of fire during dry summer weather when sparks from your fireplace may give you concern, you can control this by placing a wire screen on top of your chimney flue. Weigh it down with a few small stones. If your fire burns too wildly in a situation like this, you can quickly discipline it with a cup or two of cold water.

Make It Attractive

WHILE the mechanics of outdoor fireplace construction are important, let us also put into the building a bit of simple artistry. There should be ample shelf space. A big stone slab on either side of the fire pit. Shelves near the chimney. They will serve also as warming ovens. After a little experience, you will find the right spots to keep your plates hot, another to keep the coffee

simmering. Add to this a stone seat or two. A bit of rail fence will invite birds and small animals. The stone slabs on either side of your fire pit will, with constant use, become covered with grease and pot-black and will show discoloration. This is easily removed. Simply sprinkle a thin coat of wood ashes over the greasy part. The lye in the ashes will take up the grease. Brush off and scrub as you would your kitchen sink. Your stone will sparkle again with its natural color and look most inviting.

Here we have a deluxe adaptation of the outdoor cooking place with a roof. I have seen some very elaborate housed-in cooking contraptions, which left me with the feeling, "Why after all forsake the efficient kitchen in the house?" The only advantage of a roof is in the event of a sudden rainstorm after you have gotten the meal underway. I've met this problem with an eight-foot-square canvas that can be quickly placed.

Make the outdoor stove in your yard a place where friends will gather. Place benches and garden chairs around it. They will rediscover cooking is not drudgery, but an art of creating delectables. Here is the place to create new dishes according to your own ideas. Try cooking with olive oil—you'll like it. Try okra or eggplant; try different spices. Your friends will be attracted. Recipes and new dishes will be shared.

What makes an out-of-doors meal is, first of all, the out of doors. The very setting is important. Floating clouds, the call of wildlife, birds overhead—the smell of pungent pines wafting past you and through you. Have you ever woken up refreshed after a good night's sleep out in the open and eaten sourdough pancakes as only an old prospector in the Rockies can bake them? Let's have breakfast with one of these old sourdoughs. The delicate sizzling noise of frying bacon, sputtering eggs, the rich aroma of coffee simmering in its blackened coffee pot. It does something to you. An occasional whiff of smoke from the campfire and a stack of golden brown sourdough cakes. I still thrill to that morning years ago camping on Cripple Creek in Colorado, when Harry E. Moreland, that grand old camper-prospector, yelled, "The burnt offering is now served!"

To prepare such a meal over the campfire, with a nicety, without smearing pot-black over one's face and clothes, will add to the art of living happily in the out of doors.

Outdoor Cookery in the Garden Fireplace

COOKING in your garden fireplace is not only fun, it's getting back to nature. It is a real art. For perfect family companionship and participation there is nothing in this world that will give you and yours more satisfaction, the sense of accomplishment, and satisfaction after it is done with, than a family-cooked royal meal prepared in your outdoor garden fireplace.

If you want your friends to come often, try the out-of-doors cooking party. They won't come just to eat. You will have created a new and intriguing situation. Your friends will say, "When do we have another? We'll bring the steaks— we'll bring anything you say, but let's have another garden dinner party."

A few simple suggestions before you start your meal:

1. Take with you to your cooking "den" all needed equipment.

2. Have sufficient wood for the fire (three arms' full or more).

3. Be sure to include a good axe and a low box or table with a cover.

4. Be sure your fire burns long enough to build up a good bed of coals. Replenish your fire three times with hardwood if you want hot coals—and really hot coals are the secret of a successfully cooked outdoor meal. Please don't make the common error of cooking over flames. They only blacken your pots, give unsteady heat—first burning your food and often leaving it half cooked, underdone—faugh!

5. Take with you a towel and, if you can, a basin of water and soap. This will help make you a clean outdoor cook and keep your clothes clean throughout.

6. Include a few old newspapers, especially if you must put your steak grill on the grass, as well as kettles of vegetables and other food-stuffs. When through, burn the paper and destroy any evidence of untidiness.

7. Be sure to bring salt and pepper shakers, a long fork, and necessary utensils for your meal. You will spoil the dignity of your attempted culinary art if you have to run back to the kitchen for this or that.

HOW DO YOU LIKE YOUR STEAK?
Rare
Medium
Well Done
Roasted

Now let's have a one-inch steak for our party tonight. This calls for a bit of argument with the butcher. You prefer tenderloin, T-bone, sirloin? You want it so thick? How long has it been cured? Soon the butcher will meet your requirements. It finds its way into your icebox until the appointed hour. In all my experience of broiling steaks to make them just really perfect when served, this calls for one sure approach. No matter how badly you cook your steak, no matter how much it is overdone or underdone, you won't go far wrong at any time if you are sure your butcher gave you really good steaks. If it comes out right and the steak is delicious, take full credit for it. Chances are, you won't deserve the credit until you have learned to select a good steak.

Broiling steak is as old as time, yet many steaks could be better if a few simple precautions were taken. I prefer a one-inch steak. Thicker steaks, say two inches, are hard to broil in an outdoor fireplace unless you have had long experience.

When we talk of rare steak, do we mean red inside? Dripping in blood? Not for me. The rare steak, to my taste, should have had the effect of the coals heating it to a thorough hot throughout. If you like your steak raw, better serve it raw and call it such.

Place your steaks in a toaster grill. Put one-half-inch strips of bacon across the steak at three-inch intervals and at right angles to the wire of your grill. Bacon enriches the flavor. Place the grill on your bed of hot coals. (Put a half-brick at the far side of your coals and a fresh green log nearest you on which to rest the grill.) The grill should be about two inches from the coals. Let it sizzle for two minutes. Then turn the steaks over. Listen to the grease drip into the hot coals. Watch it jump into the flames. Good! Let it burn. Let the flames play around the steaks for about three minutes *wildly!* Turn the steaks over and repeat. If flames do not start at once, throw in a shaving. (Have you a jackknife? It counts in broiling a good steak.) After three more minutes of "wild" burning of your steak, you will have a perfect one—burnt brown on the outside, juicy and rare within. For your guests who want well-done steaks, just roast them a bit longer. Add salt and pepper and top with butter before serving.

The meal over with, you will soon start singing folksongs, chatting, singing again. Someone brings a guitar or banjo. Soon there are blinking stars. Again a lovely night. In season, we find lovely, inspiring nights in any part of this global world. Let's use them. Call in your guests, your friends, for a supper about your outdoor garden fireplace.

HAMBURGERS

I've grown thoroughly dissatisfied with the modern hamburgers as served by most food shops. To begin with, they come paper-thin—almost as thin as the oilpaper sheets that separate them. They are then almost burned to a crisp, cooked through and through, and served with hot sauces to cover the lack of natural flavor. Beef, to me, must always be rare at its heart. Try rare hamburgers. First buy good beef and have it chopped. Make it into small balls or fat patties two inches thick. Put a little butter into the frying pan. Be sure your fire is *hot*. Fry vigorously for two minutes. Flatten slightly. Turn, season, and repeat. Your hamburger is ready to serve. It is as good as a choice steak—costs less and is most simple to prepare. It's fun!

HUNTER'S STEW

If you want to serve a meal to a large group without spending half of next month's earnings, try Kettle-Hole Hunter's Stew. It is easily prepared and makes a satisfying meal. It's unique and different.

Let's say you are to have ten or fifteen folks for Sunday supper. Buy boneless meat—beef, lamb, pork—or all three. Allow six ounces per person. Bones will add to the richness and flavor but should not be counted on as fillers. Cut the meat into small pieces and drop into hot salted water. You will not have to watch your Kettle-Hole Stew, but can return after two hours and find it ready to serve. Here's how.

Dig a hole about eighteen inches deep and six inches wider than the diameter of your cooking utensil. We use a ten-quart pail with a lid. Be sure the walls of the pit are straight up and down. Now set a crotched stick on either side of the hole. Across these lay a green pole. Hang the pail on the crosspole so it is half way down into the hole. Before placing the pail, build a good fire in the hole. Let it burn until a bed of live coals has accumulated. Now place your pail, filled three-quarters full of water. Next, build a stockade fence of three-foot-long branches (about one to three inches in thickness) around the pail. See that the lower ends of these branches are resting in the coals below. Your fire is now self-feeding.

When the water boils, salt it and add your

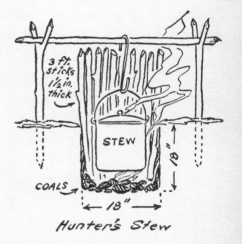

Hunter's Stew

meat. Cover the pail and then leave it alone. Bring out the camp chairs and cushions and savor the fragrance of your stew. Control your appetite. Just a half-hour before serving, add vegetables—potatoes, carrots, celery, onions, seasoning. When all is ready, ladle out a cup of broth, add a crisp salad, bread and butter, a light dessert, coffee. You'll like it. Your guests will go home well fed and happy, and will be eager to try this easy meal in their own backyards.

POTATOES BAKED IN A HOLE

The earth must be sandy and reasonably dry. Potatoes will bake brown and mealy in fifty-five minutes in a fire hole. Dig the hole eighteen inches deep by fourteen inches wide. Build a fire of hardwood. Let it burn until the hole is half-full of coals. With a shovel push the coals aside, then throw in a layer of potatoes. Quickly release the shovel and the potatoes will be covered with hot coals. Now fill in the hole with the loose dirt that has been dug out from the hole. The potatoes cannot char, but will come out brown and mealy.

Another way is to wrap the potatoes in clay and bake them in the coals of a campfire. About the same amount of time is required. A few experiments are necessary to prove this skill.

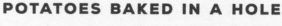

NEW ENGLAND BOILED DINNER

Just which of the New England states would claim discovery of this richly flavored meal, I do not know. It came to me from our Vermont relatives and shared the honors with Boston Baked Beans and Brown Bread as a Saturday night repast.

The unit is a lean rump of freshly corned beef. It is covered with cold water and set to simmer in a large covered kettle. After an hour or so (depending, of course, on the weight of the piece), the vegetables are added. First (because they take most time), add golden slices of turnip or rutabaga. Then add quarters of young cabbage, about three large onions, and as many whole potatoes as desired. No further salt or seasoning is necessary. Now, in a separate kettle set to simmer until tender, cook plenty of fresh red beets. Cook them with their jackets on to preserve their deep-red color. Serve these separately. (Don't peel the beets with a knife. As soon as they are cool enough to handle, their jackets can be gently squeezed off.)

"RED FLANNEL" HASH

After your New England dinner, drain all vegetables thoroughly. Remove the corned beef. Add to the drained vegetables the peeled beets. Place in a wooden chopping bowl. Chop fine and mix thoroughly. Let stand overnight and serve for breakfast. Just heat thoroughly in a buttered frying pan or skillet. This meal has become a standard Sunday morning breakfast with us.

CHILI

There is one meal we like to serve on any occasion, where food and simple preparation are the two points most of focus. It is the kind of a meal, too, that can be stretched almost indefinitely. It is easily carried, easily salvaged. It is a one-dish meal with all the needed food elements. Its preparation need take a mere twenty minutes and, yet, what is often more important in a mixed group of varied plans and interests, it never spoils by a delay in serving.

The unit ingredients serve five. Into an iron-covered kettle, place one pound of hamburger. Cover it and let it sear rather than brown. Add one large can of tomatoes, one jar of prepared kidney beans, one can of spaghetti in spicy sauce. Add a heaping teaspoon of salt. Stir well and let it heat through. Just before serving, add two tablespoons of chili powder.

If the group number has not been determined before the purchase of supplies, double the amount of hamburger, triple the number of cans, and all is set for most any contingency, provided the kettle space is adequate. Add a quarter-pound

of hamburger and one can of any of the ingredients for each additional guest. Somehow, though the flavor may be varied slightly in one direction or another, it won't ruin the nourishing and appetizing result. The unopened cans, even the unused hamburger, can be utilized for other meals without waste.

BAKED BEANS

Here is a bit of outdoor bean cookery that works. Beans are put to soak overnight and then boiled until tender. They are then placed in a stone jar with a cover. The jar is then filled with chunks of salt pork, syrup, and spice to suit one's taste. For an oven, use a five-gallon tin can with the top removed, or a piece of sheet iron the height of the stone jar and about three feet long, bent into a circle to fit around the jar. Cover the top with a piece of flat tin. A slow-burning fire built around the tin cover is the last step, except to dip into the jar from time to time to taste and to keep enough water on the beans to prevent burning. But "what a meal" when the pork and beans are served!

THE "HOT DOG, BACON, AND MELTED CHEESE DREAM"

For a simple picnic meal at little cost but big returns, try a "Hot Dog, Bacon, and Melted

Cheese Dream." Wieners or hot dogs, one or more for each member in the party, split in half lengthwise. Place within a thin slice of American cheese. Now slit a strip of bacon lengthwise and roll the half piece around the wiener like a barber's pole. Place it in a reflector oven and roast. After a few minutes of broiling, turn the wieners around to roast on the other side. After another eight minutes, your meat and cheese "dreams" are ready—cheese melted and oozing out. Have the buns or bread toasted and hot, add a pot of coffee or tea, and here you have a tasty picnic meal. Add radishes, celery, or olives. (Helps with the roughage.) Now a bit of fruit or the added homemade pie. Yum, yum.

Burn up the paper plates and cups and go home with no worry about dishwashing. Reflect on a perfect day and you haven't ruined your pocketbook. Every meal need not be a banquet. The fun of eating includes companionship, working together, the sparkle of the fireplace, cooling embers, and confidences.

CHEESE AND CRACKERS

Brown the crackers in the fireplace reflector oven. When slightly brown, put a thin slice of cheese between two crackers. Roast for a few minutes. The cheese will run over, under, and around the crackers. Serve hot and boast, "It can't be beat!" Good for late afternoon with a cup of tea—or perhaps a bit "wild," but mild, hot buttered rum—but that's another story.

FIREPLACE CINNAMON TOAST

For a four o'clock tidbit, there is nothing equal to toasted white bread with cinnamon and sugar. First, toast the bread. Then, spread it with butter, sprinkle with cinnamon, and spread with sugar. Set it back against the fire 'til the sugar gets hot and sizzles and the cinnamon spreads—your toast is ready. Add a cup of tea or coffee. It's a perfect four o'clock treat. Your guests will like it.

ROLLED ROAST OF BEEF

Before the fireplace or open fire . . . roast beef, either rib or rolled, needs constant turning before a reflector fire. Bind the roast with stove-pipe wire, both ways, to hold it tightly together. Have one lead wire running up from the roast and fasten to a piece of twine or cord. This is to provide for twisting. Fasten the twine to the top of the fireplace shelf or on a pole in front of your open fire. On the twine above the wire, place a cross-stick, ends of which run through the cord strand. These rest against the fireplace wall. Turn this stick every five or ten minutes so the roast is exposed on all sides. With an outdoor

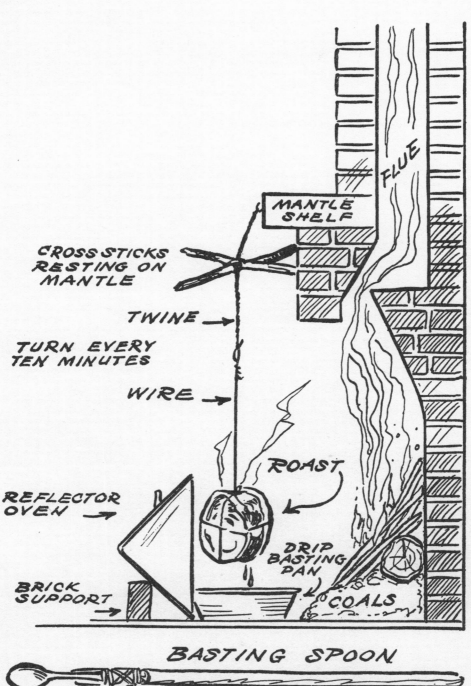

FLUE

MANTLE SHELF

CROSS STICKS RESTING ON MANTLE

TWINE →

TURN EVERY TEN MINUTES

WIRE →

ROAST

REFLECTOR OVEN →

DRIP BASTING PAN

BRICK SUPPORT →

COALS

BASTING SPOON

WOOD HANDLE — 3 FT. LONG

fire, a longer branch, say three feet long, can be applied to regulate the turning of the roast.

I forgot to mention the drip pan. Place a frying pan below the roast just in front of the reflector oven. (See sketch.) Place in this drip pan a bit of lemon, orange juice, cinnamon, cloves, butter, sugar, and water enough to keep it watery. Soon the roast will begin to sizzle and drip into the drip pan below. With a long-handled spoon (fasten a three-foot wooden handle to a large tureen spoon) dip up the juice from the drip pan and baste the hot roast every few minutes. Flames will flare up. Keep a hot fire. Don't worry. This is as it should be. Keep the fire very hot. An eight-pound roast will require about two hours. Gather around the fireplace—cushions, chairs, perhaps a bridge game—but watch the roast. Keep basting often.

When is it done? If you want a rare roast inside and burnt and crisp on the outside, the preceding will show you the way. The best way to really know is to cook a few roasts of your own. You will finally find your own answer—rare, medium, well done, burnt—or all at the same time.

BOTTOM TRAY

THE SHORE DINNER

Do you really want a great meal full of anticipation? A meal that will keep you drooling for forty-five minutes as you watch its progress? A meal, which, in its stages of development, will make you forget business, problems, worries, and, when finished and eaten, will leave you relaxed and in a happy daze of comfortable calm? A meal fit for kings, but which today may be enjoyed by vagabonds?

226

Are you really hungry, and are you prepared to intrigue your palate with a real rare experience, which, after eating, will leave your satiated, contented, satisfied? Then try the Lobster Pot—lobsters, clams, clam broth, chicken, vegetables—all in one cooker the size of the family wash boiler. Indeed, the home wash boiler is just about right size to cook for a party of up to ten people.

It is obvious being four to five hundred miles from the seashore (Buffalo, New York), we must secure the best and freshest lobsters and clams possible. Through an arrangement I have with a Boston shipper, we get lobsters delivered here in Buffalo within fifteen hours after being caught.

The meal is a perfectly simple one, or it can be made elaborate. It is not an expensive meal. Most of all it needs a little dramatics—the out-of-door setting, the group near enough to the outdoor cooking to watch it casually as conversation leads to western civilization, war, peace, and humdrum gossip. But observe all of the food items that are included—the stunning of the lobsters by a blow on the head and puncturing the brain with an ice pick—not pleasant but humane—green, fresh, live lobsters that come out of the pot a brilliant red.

The spigot on the lobster pot is not essential, but very convenient, for the first course is the serving of a cup of broth together with a big bowl of clams and drawn butter. Serve each person wherever they are sitting—on the grass, in garden chairs, etc. If the broth is really as it should be—that is, made up of all the drippings from the food within the cooker, your guests will want a second helping. So they go over to the cooker and draw from the spigot the steaming broth, without having to dip down deep into the cooker and risk the danger of burns from the steam.

Because I could not find the kind of equipment I wanted for my shore dinner, I had my own tank or lobster pot cooker made. It is nothing more than a tin tank, 16 inches by 16 inches by 16 inches, with a somewhat snug-fitting cover. Within are four wire basket trays that fit one on top of the other. They contain all the ingredients except bread, butter, salad, coffee, and dessert.

Here is what to include—clams, lobsters, chicken (if you want to be lavish), celery, carrots, potatoes, sweet corn, green or wax beans, or any combination of fresh vegetables, and seaweed. The broth, clams, and lobsters are the important part of the meal. You won't want to eat many vegetables—their importance is to flavor the broth.

But let's get on with the preparation—

1. Pour a gallon and a half of water into the cooker. Bring to a wild boiling state—that is, there must be real steam generated in the cooker to the point where the cover will bob up and down and may need a small stone on top to keep it in place.

2. Place the lobsters (preferably two-pound ones) in the second tray from the bottom; cover with seaweed.

3. Wrap each piece of chicken in cheesecloth. When the dinner is done, the chicken should be white and mealy and will need to be pan-browned in butter. The cheesecloth will keep the meat from falling apart. Place the cut-up chicken (broilers are preferable) in the next tray above. If there is any room in the tray, add vegetables. Note: The chicken is an extra and can be omitted.

4. In the next tray above, put the rest of the vegetables. Sweet corn on the cob is most desirable and will do much to enrich the broth. (Note: Speaking of these trays, I have attached to the bottom tray a long wire handle running up on the inside of either side of the cooker so all trays can be lifted out at one time. A good pair of canvas gloves with cuffs is necessary to protect your hands and arms from the steam.)

5. Put these four trays in the cooker and let them steam for forty minutes. And, I mean steam!

6. At the end of the forty minutes, lift out all trays and fill the bottom tray with clams. Put all trays back and steam for ten minutes longer. Your shore dinner will then be ready.

7. Remove the cooker from the fire. Draw off the broth. Serve a bowl of clams to your guests with dishes of drawn butter. Eat the clams with your fingers and have plenty of towels or paper napkins on hand. Be prepared to decorate your face from ear to ear. One just may not be fastidious at this stage of the game.

8. In the meantime, place the trays on a table or bench and let your guests help themselves. It will be necessary, however, for someone to split the lobsters into halves after you have removed the seaweed. This is best done with a small hand-axe or cleaver, if you have one. One-half lobster to each person is ample.

9. Now add a chef's salad, bread, butter, coffee, and those other things you may want for your meal. For dessert, there is nothing I have found that goes better than just half a grapefruit. It cuts through and brings one back to normal.

If you go to a cottage where you have tables, dishes, and all of the other equipment, then, of course, it is nice to serve this shore dinner with a bit more formality. As I said in the beginning, there is nothing unusual about this meal. Be sure to get seaweed when you buy your lobsters. Do not salt the chicken or you will spoil the tang of the seaweed. Seaweed will season it sufficiently. The chicken should be salted to taste when browned.

Another tip. Be sure to watch your broth so it does not boil away. You will have to determine the amount of water by the size of the cooker you have at your disposal. To me, the best part of the meal is the clam broth. Save the leftover broth for lunch tomorrow.

FRONT

REFLECTOR-OVEN BISCUITS

Do you know how to mix baking powder biscuits without using utensils and measuring tools? No? Let me give you an outdoor 1-4-3-2-1 method.

Take a handful of flour (as much as your cupped hand will hold). Put it in a dish, or small pail, if you do this at home. If on a hike, put it in a washed five-pound salt bag. Now dip your fingers and thumb, drawn to a point, into the baking powder can and draw out as much baking powder as your fingers and thumb will hold. It won't be much, but it will be enough. Next pick up as much salt as you can pick up with three fingers and your thumb and throw into the "kitty" (bag). Your next move is to pick up all the sugar you can with two fingers and the thumb. Add this to the bag. Finally, stick your index finger into a jar of shortening and withdraw as much as you can up to the first knuckle. You now have the ingredients for one big biscuit. If you want two or more, increase the process to the size and number of biscuits you want. Add milk or, if milk is not available, water and mix to a stiff paste. Sprinkle a bit of flour on a piece of paper, flatten your biscuit, and cut into inch-and-a-half squares. Place them in the reflector oven pan and place the reflector oven close to the hot fire. After a few minutes, turn the biscuits around to bake on both sides. Now get a real taste of the sunny south. Serve with butter and jam.

PERPETUAL PANCAKES

Ingredients: 3 cups of buckwheat flour, ½ teaspoon salt, 1 yeast cake (in first mixing), 2 cups buttermilk, sour milk, or water, 1 teaspoon baking soda.

This unit can be varied according to the number of pancakes desired. There should be at least a cupful of batter left as a starting unit for the next day. Again, add milk, flour, or cornmeal.

CORN PONES (FOR EIGHT PEOPLE)

Ingredients: 3 cups yellow cornmeal, 1 cup flour, 1 teaspoon salt, 8 teaspoons baking powder, 2 teaspoons sugar, 4 cups water.

Combine the dry ingredients and the shortening. Stir in enough water to be able to drop the mixture from a spoon.

To bake: (1) Fill a pan ½-inch deep and place it in the reflector oven; or,

(2) put the batter in a frying pan, ¼-inch thick, and hold over the fire to bake the bottom. Then, bake the top by reflector heat—propping the pan against the fire; or (3) drop spoonfuls on a very hot rock.

YOUR COMPLETE DINNER ON TWO STICKS OF WOOD

A delicious meal can be cooked on two sticks of wood. Beef, mutton, or lamb—onion, bacon, biscuits, plus potatoes baked in the coals, a cup of cocoa, and an apple—a real meal, without any cooking utensils—just a cup for the cocoa. Do you want to try it in your garden? Well, I have explained the importance of a good bed of coals, which is vital in any outdoor pioneer-cooking venture.

This meal is simple. Cut a straight branch of dry wood, preferably white pine, the thickness of your thumb and about two feet long. Some wood is bitter (like oak), some sweet. The way to find out is to taste it. If it tastes bitter, then certainly it isn't sweet—so avoid it. With your jackknife, whittle your stick smooth and cut a sharp point at one end.

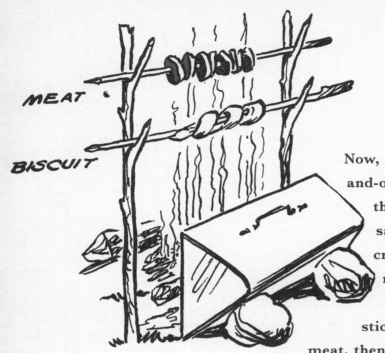

MEAT

BISCUIT

Now, cut your meat into one-and-one-half-inch squares. Cut the bacon slices to the same size. Cut the onions crosswise so you will have many rings. Next, push the pointed end of the stick through a piece of meat, then a piece of bacon, then a ring of onion. Do this again and again until you have at least a quarter-pound of meat or more, according to your appetite—first meat, then bacon, then onion until the stick is filled. Leave an eighth-inch of space between each piece. Salt and pepper. (If you really want a pioneer salt and pepper shaker, take a piece of your old bamboo fishing pole. Cut off two inches on either side of the joint. Fill one end with salt, the other with pepper. Put a cork in each end and put it in your pocket until needed.)

Now we come to the real fun. Prepare the biscuit using the 1-4-3-2-1 method as previously explained. Secure another stick like the one for your meat. Flatten your biscuit batter into a long ribbon about two inches wide and about eight inches long and one-half inch thick. Wind this around the second stick, barber pole fashion, and pinch tight at either end of the stick to seal it in place.

Start to bake your potatoes first, because they take longer. Put them deep into the coals or use the reflector oven. They take about forty minutes and time is important if you want to serve everything hot.

Cut two branches about two feet long with small branches sticking out at the side and tip to hold your two sticks. (See illustration.) Force these into the ground on either side of the hot coals. Place the meat stick on the top crotch. Give it a quarter turn every five minutes. Soon it will begin to sizzle. The fat from the bacon will run into the beef and the onion will curl and brown and flavor your meat. Now place your biscuit stick on the crotch below and, likewise, give it a quarter turn every few minutes. Soon it will begin to swell and then brown. (Stop drooling! Wait a bit longer.) Next, the juice from the meat and bacon above will drip down on your biscuit and you will have a buttered hot biscuit.

Set your cup of cocoa near the fire, unwrap the celery and radishes, shine up the apple for your dessert, and—presto—you have prepared a royal meal.

Throw all the waste into the fire,
Take home the cup and now aspire
To simpler life and greater giving.
You, too, will grow by simple living.

Picnic a la "Cart"

TRY out your guests on a party picnic a la "cart." This is a small, two-wheeled cart with an icebox, storage room for food, fixings, and cooking gear. All spaces are arranged for the picnic feed. Make it yourself. I made mine and it works. It is different.

Two drop-leaf tables that fold on top when open give ample serving space. You don't have to go to your backyard fireplace every time you want an outdoor meal. If on a stream or lake, or at the seashore, have a shore dinner—clams, lobsters. Start with clam broth or soup. Try hot dogs or a New England dinner with vegetables.

If you have a favorite spot, a view from a hilltop, a sunset—perhaps a swim—then load your picnic a la "cart" with food, drinks, and gear and have a hilltop meal with an inspirational view. It will give you a different setting. Your friends will like it and beg to come again.

Picnic a la "cart" is a country home variety to your place in the woods. It's just a stunt, but different. It is the "tea tray" in your living room, a bit roughed up. It's fun. It's novel. Add a few cushions, a campfire, songs, stunts, the moon, twinkling stars . . . a perfect party.

Great
Out Doors

OUR pioneer fathers learned the art of living happily together in God's Out Doors. No running water. No electric lights. No radios. No automobiles. No servants. They lived simply—clear in thinking, clean in relationships, hard fighting, but friendly to a fault to a neighbor in distress. They lived by simple standards, asked little of life, were willing to work hard, and contented with meager returns. Occasionally they relaxed. When they were playful they "played hard, and when they worked they didn't play at all."

Life is different today. It's easier in many ways, but it is tense and highly geared. It plays on our nervous system. It does not contribute to wholesome fatigue at the end of a day as the fatigue of a day of simple hard labor—sweat, wholesome toil, physical things—accomplished.

We of today have not changed much. Our environment has changed. We still have it in our blood to "revert to the land," to the out of doors. And just so, because of the pattern of city life we need again to learn, as our ancestors did, the art of living happily together in the woods. In a word, going back somewhat to primitive thinking and living, simple pleasures, homely tasks. It calls for a release from the urge of going to the movies, nightclubs—late hours, continuous excitement as a steady diet—all of which is the result of restlessness, and restlessness is often the result of overexcitement and too much stimulation.

In our Cabin in the Woods, contentment may come from the quiet of friends around our fireside, neighborhood news, storytelling, companionship, the enjoyment of a good book, or, unashamed, we crawl into bed at the "ridiculous" hour of half past eight or nine o'clock.

Let us get still closer to the outdoors by living for a spell in a tent. Perhaps we can clarify a bit how we can come to better understand and enjoy the outdoors by a mere intimate knowledge and understanding of outdoor life, of the relationship of ourselves to the elements, to wildlife, to those folks about us—simple living.

To live successfully out of doors, no matter if one is thirty, fifty, or more, one needs a reasonable feeling of security. Added to this, we need experience in outdoor living that will prove or disprove the things we have learned of the out of doors. Next, the urgent need of friendliness and understanding—friendliness with those about us, of wild animal life about us that brings happiness to us and security to them. Finally, we all need approval and satisfaction. Approval from those about us. Satisfaction in a job well done. To do so we need an outdoor setting. Will you and your family, therefore, go with me and mine to our favorite camp spot and camp in tents for a few days? Let's be primitive. It is June. New York State. Tents, duffel, and equipment are all packed. A short thirty-mile trip and we are out in the woods— alone and away from the world. We have chosen the spot. Soon tents are up. The outdoor kitchen with pots, pans, and improvised stove is all set. We are away for a long weekend on our own.

Now we must change from city togs to those of the out of doors. Let's be comfortable. A red shirt, colorful corduroy trousers or slacks, shirt open at the neck.

This is lovely countryside. Nothing majestic, just rolling hills, valleys, trees, farms, fences—a small lake. We can see, as our hillside slopes down to the small lake below, scattered stately trees, elms, maples—especially one that stands alone and has spread its great branches, massive, proud, commanding. There are meadows about, bushes, young trees growing strong. Bushy trees shade our tents. The tree stump nearby will serve as a feeding station for the squirrel and chipmunk playing hide-and-seek among the rocks and trees. See, they are looking us over. The spring-fed stream just beside our camp flows quietly. From the dugout pool comes a constant supply of sweet, fresh drinking water for our needs.

The small lake below us is fringed with trees. A few tents on the far side add contentment, for we know there, too, are lovers of the out of doors. Out of hearing distance, they add to the setting. A bright-green upturned canoe on the sandy beach is clearly visible. The day is sunny and warm. Still. Serene.

Beyond the lake, the land rises upward for several miles until it reaches the great skyline, dotted with trees, farms, forests. The hillside is laid out in great patches of farmlands, each surrounded by fences, some still with picturesque old-fashioned rail fences. Each plot is fringed with bushes, trees. To the right is the cow pasture—green—where contented cattle spend lazy long days. Far to the right is the great balsam swamp. We must make a trip there someday. It is really a bird sanctuary.

In the middle of all this setting are our neighboring farmer's house, barns, silos, garden spots, and orchards. The Moores are hardworking folks. They live simply. They have no need to envy city folks. They are the salt of the earth and the backbone of our democracy.

So I welcome you to enjoy with me this lovely countryside.

Security: The North Woods

NOW that our camp is all set, let's sit down for a heart-to-heart talk. Let's talk about the art of living happily together in the woods.

What do we mean by "security in the out of doors"? Is it self-preservation? Or, is it accepting nature happily and living without mental reservations?

My daughter and I once made a canoe trip into Canadian waters. On arrival at a waystation, we loaded our duffel into our canoe and paddled several miles down Pickerel River, stopping for breakfast with friends. It was raining hard. They wanted us to stay with them because of the wet weather. My daughter, after thanking them, turned to me and said, "Daddy, let's camp. We can take it." So we paddled on. We found an island to set up our camp and it became our island. We took one- or two-day trips from our island camp. One day on returning, we paddled nearly twenty miles. It was a stormy rainy day. It was a hard pull against the strong headwind. Late in the afternoon, I asked my daughter whether she was getting tired. "No," she said and paddled on. I was grateful she didn't ask me. At last, we found our island and our tent camp. We unloaded our duffel and, dripping wet, hurried to our tent. We quickly started a cheery reflector fire from dry wood stored within our tent. A change to dry linen, a good supper, and my daughter sat back and said, "Daddy, isn't this snug?" She was really saying she enjoyed the security of a companion who could "take it." Security in that Great Out Doors—miles from the nearest supply station and, yet, there we were, happy, comfortable, with the feeling we could take care of ourselves in those faraway primitive conditions and enjoy it. That is a bit of real security.

All of us who live in the woods need mental security. I wish I could, by a miracle, relieve all folks who, through their childhood days, had their lives spoiled by superstition, inhibitions, fears—those things that have gripped them and distorted their thinking because of misinformation. Do you still hesitate when a black cat crosses your path?

FEAR

I have been in many "tight" places in the Rockies, the Canadian woods, and streams when fear gripped me to the point where mental processes ceased suddenly to be rational. Environmental influence can play tricks with one's thinking.

Once while "shooting" swift rapids, my canoe shipped water. The going was tough—"can't make it"—fear—fright—then panic gripped me. "Help! Help!" But there was no one within miles. I pictured myself dead—stiff and cold at the bottom of the falls miles below. I hate water in my nose . . . . My last will and testament—what will happen to my new camping equipment?

This kind of thing comes with lightning speed. Fear grips you and strangles the ability to think sanely. Do something—attack and your fear begins to give way. Take a firm grip on your paddle and say over and over again, "I won't give up. I won't give up. I can make it. I will."

I've been lost on the trail. "The compass is 'cockeyed.' It points the wrong way." I started to run. Crazy? Of course. You're really not lost. You're just confused. Get a hold on yourself. Sit down on a log. Take a deep breath and look around. Gradually, your tension lessens and normal thinking brings a returned faith in your compass and, eventually, the way back to the trail.

Fear keeps close companionship with doubt, flirts with misinformation, encourages lack of self-confidence, welcomes superstition, inconsistency, and goes hand in hand with worry. Fear is the hobgoblin of confused thinking. It comes from within. Grandmother used to say, "It's in you what ails you." I believe she's right. What ails you and what cures you are within you. Even night noises, stealthy footfalls, the panic of seeing a snake too suddenly—all met by thought or built into "mountains" by worry. "It's in you what ails you."

AT HOME IN THE FOREST

Did you ever have that empty feeling when by yourself in the deep woods, when eerie noises from the wildlife, the movement of trees and bushes gave you a bit of jitters and the sense of utter aloneness? I have lived through that experience but have outgrown it. Now the woods are full of friendliness. I have learned to know the wildlife by name, and nature and noises that have simple homely meanings. The squirrel scolds. The chipmunk chirps. The crow calls, "caw, caw, caw," a rally or a warning.

Look about you. You will discover three worlds teeming with abundant life. Beneath you—the underground world—small holes in the earth, home and security to hundreds of small

animals. A world from which man is barred. Back doors and front doors, storage rooms and communication tunnels. Then there is a world for the long-legs that depend on speed for their livelihood. They step noiselessly, creep stealthily, or crash boldly through the trails or brush, according to their natures. The fox, the wolf, the deer—not often seen by one who has never learned the art of stalking, who cannot avoid snapping twigs, who "telegraphs" ahead of his approach as he brushes and stirs dry leaves in passing.

The third world is that of the treetops and the sky. Here, squirrels use the interwoven branches as their natural thoroughfare. Songbirds flit from tree to tree, hawks circle and swoop, wild geese in patterned flight thread seemingly charted paths across the dark blue ocean of the sky.

Man is never alone in the woods. Even at night, you can see the gleam of tiny eyes watching you, fearful, ever alert. The satisfying triumph of their confidence in you is worth the time and patience it takes to win it.

LOST AND FOUND

Being lost in either the woods or the city, or anywhere else for that matter, can be largely attributed to just plain ignorance. The uninformed get lost. The would-be sailor who takes a sailboat out in a light breeze becomes "lost" when the fog descends and he realizes he is not wise in the ways of the water.

Being lost is closely allied to being confused. Confusion comes from lack of pertinent information. How often we meet people who join in discussions "over their heads" and find themselves utterly "lost" because they were misinformed or uninformed.

But let's talk of being lost in the woods. When one loses one's sense of direction, one becomes confused, then frantic and apt to do silly things. To cringe in the presence of a black snake is to be "lost" in the woods. To know good snakes from bad is to know a black snake is as tame and playful as a kitten. It is an unwise man who tampers with wild mushrooms. Many have paid the full price for ignorance.

When in doubt, sit down on a log, take time, and bring your best reasoning to bear. You will soon get your bearing. A good woodsman entering a thick woods stops occasionally to look back, realizing the way in and the way out will have different landmarks. He breaks a branch here and there. Leaves a stone or two at a turning point in the trail; watches the treetops and notes each out-of-the-ordinary landmark.

ANIMALS AND INSECTS

Let us try sleeping out on the grass in the open. Along about two o'clock in the morning, could you lie there peacefully, realizing suddenly you had a visit from a skunk who sniffled all around you? A skunk is really one of the nicest little pets and has been unfairly accused over these years. He will come to your bed because he is just a curious fellow. He is getting acquainted and has the cutest little sniffle. After looking you over, he will quietly amble off without harming you. I warn you, however, if you reach for a gun or an axe, the polecat will "shoot" first. Go to sleep, my friend, and feel secure in the thought that the polecat is your friend, too.

How many of us step on a spider as he crosses our path? Do we do it because we have added to God's great scheme of things and reduced the several billions of spiders by one? Or are we stepping on it to relieve some innate fear of ours—the fear that something might bite us? That's mental insecurity. I have known a mother whose little boy proudly showed her a great big toad, which he carried in his hand. She stiffened, withdrew, tensed—and gave him as his reward the assurance he would have a handful of warts.

What I do want to say is real security comes in the knowledge that God is in his heaven and has organized his great universe for our good. He has given you and me the privilege of being on it to enjoy it.

Years ago, I met a man who had an uncanny dislike for mosquitoes, bugs, beetles, and all creepy and crawling things. It was more than a dislike. He was fraught with fear. He termed them all insects—things unnecessary in the world, things to be despised. He was the product of misinformation in his early days. Then someone brought a change in his life. He met a naturalist in whom he had confidence. They sat on the grass on a dark night with several others. The naturalist lit a small candle and placed it in the damp grass, and said to the group as we circled about, "I'm going to show you a new world of insect life in which each has a purpose in the great scheme of the universe." We were fascinated. We forgot ourselves. With a long, thin, stick the naturalist pointed to each of the strange creatures as it crawled toward the light. A small bug crawled laboriously to the top of a blade of grass only to drop to the ground and then crawl up the next—always toward the light. Long spindly legged mosquitoes hovered over the flame. June bugs harmlessly jumped and flew with a force past the candle and would stop with a thud against one of us. Millers moths would flit about. It was like going to a miniature circus or zoo. We were so deeply interested we did not even notice the hum of an occasional mosquito. Well, neither did our pioneer fathers.

My friend with the fears and inhibitions had a rebirth and an understanding in which he became a part and accepted, at least in part, this wildlife of the outdoors. He said finally, "It's all in the way you look at it." It gave him a mental readjustment, a new evaluation, released him from many foolish fears, gave him an added security, and, finally, made him a decidedly better camping partner. This is not so easy to achieve in later life. Unless you, too, learn to accept this wildlife, you will constantly be in conflict with yourself.

There are a squirrel and chipmunk flitting about our camp. They wonder who we are. Let's get acquainted. Put a bit of food on the nearby tree stump. The chipmunk will sneak up cautiously on the far side of the stump, blink one eye, and seem to say, "Well, I'm going to try you out." The squirrel will grab his morsel and retire to a more secure spot, sit on his haunches and eat greedily while watching us. They are going to be our good friends before we get through with this camp; so will the birds and other wildlife.

Experience

SO much for security. Let us now discuss the value of experience in which we can prove the information we have been given as true, or possibly disprove the misinformation from people who just do not know God's Out Doors. True that experience is a wonderful teacher, yet we must remember in dealing with the outdoors, nature is relentless and exacts a costly price for ignorance.

CAUTION

If camping on our own, obviously we must be our own "doctor, baker, and candlestick maker." We must look after our own bodily needs and safety. If we are to enjoy our experience to the fullest, we must do all things based on correct information—but better still, on plain "horse sense," sound judgment.

Should we unwittingly drink from a stagnant pool of polluted water and discover during the night a bit of a stomachache or even worse as the ditty goes: "If in heaven you awaken and find you were mistaken," we will never live to tell the rest of the world of our adventure. If you love to swim and swim out beyond your depth and endurance and find you go under the water twice and can only come up once, your camping experience will not be in line with your plans and anticipation. Sound judgment must come into play in our every experience.

FOREST FIRES

Forest fires caused by natural forces can be easily controlled. It is fires caused by individual carelessness and ignorance that play havoc. Dry leaves and pine needles, inches deep, need but the slightest spark to launch a forest conflagration. Surely a person must be lost mentally and morally if he would deliberately start such destruction. He has never seen the results of fire in a forest—the flight of wildlife toward water. Water that shrinks with the heat—so their haven becomes a death trap. He has never seen beautiful proud trees denuded of branches, their trunks living red coals, turning at last to gaunt ghosts in a barren hell of charred death.

The cigarette smoker who carelessly flips his still-glowing butt from a car window, or drops it as he hikes, is a destroyer of life. He loves none but himself. He can be classed with the hunter whose inaccurate aim leaves his prey to run wounded, to die of fever and helplessness and starvation. Leo King, that great Adirondack woodsman, shocked me once when we were in the woods together. As he finished his cigarette down to the last half inch, he spit in the palm of his hand and dipped the still glowing stub into the spittle, rubbing it into nothingness before he was content to throw it away. Not a tidy procedure this? This man had once been driven before a forest fire. He had been burned in fighting forest fires. He knew and was protecting the life and forests he loved. God give us more people as thoughtful.

The casual camper is another menace to our forests. Be sure to put out your fire! If you cannot find a rock for a base, or an open spot away from deep vegetation, then do a bit of digging and have on hand buckets of water to soak the ground underneath. Better still, if you are not woods wise, build no fire in the woods, but resort to public parks where outdoor fireplaces are provided.

BAD JUDGMENT

Suppose you choose a lovely grassy spot down near a little babbling brook for your camp—a spot that looks like a perfect setting on a sunny day. You set up camp, pitch your tent, make up your bed, enjoy your campfire, retire and "wrap the draperies of your couch about you and lie down to pleasant dreams." Having gone to sleep, a quiet, slow drizzly rain starts to refresh the earth. But the overflow has been running down the hillside and into your little babbling brook. The waters have risen higher and higher—"stealing in on you like a thief in the night." Suddenly you have that embarrassing awakening to find the heaviest part of your anatomy quietly bathed by lapping waters from under your bed. So you grab your searchlight from under your pillow and have the added chagrin of finding your shoes, your coffee, canned goods, and underwear playing hide-and-seek with each other as they float about within your tent. Pray God tomorrow will be a sunny day because you will need spend all of it drying out. I am sure, next time, you will set up your tent on higher ground. This knowledge one does not get out of books. It takes experience. This is applied education.

Then there is the camper who goes out to rough it. He wants to be able to "take it." So, with a little cotton blanket and minimum equipment he rolls out on the grass and goes blissfully to sleep. Along about two o'clock in the morning he finds he is propped up on two "piers"—one nice little stone under his shoulder and one under his hips, and he spends the next day nursing what he thinks may be lumbago. So he, too, will find the value of carefully preparing a good bed if he wants a good night's sleep. Experience is a great teacher.

Weather Wise

"IT'S going to rain," says my farmer friend.
My own mind, at this point, reverts to the
upper left-hand corner of the newspaper, or to
the on-the-hour broadcast of weather reports.
These weather observers do our thinking and
interpreting for us. Thanks—but it is not enough.
We have grown dependent on clocks, bells,
whistles—mechanical devices. We have lost the
ability to read the skies and the earth. Nature
has always been full of advance information,
would we but heed it. The city has dulled our
perceptions. We idle at street crossings until
a dummy green light flashes "SAFE CROSSING." A
noon siren tells us it is time for lunch. We have
forgotten to note the sun at the zenith. We no
longer wait for that nice empty feeling in the
pit of our stomachs. School bells regulate our
children's lives. Time clocks and office hours
or bus schedules determine for us a good day's
work. What automatons we have permitted
ourselves to become!

"It's going to rain!" Of course. But you can't
see this from your office chair. I hope you need
not always feel tied to factory or office, because,
if so, your outdoor mind will grow dull. Soon
birds, wild animals, trees, and the skies that

dome over you will lose their meaning. Let us heed the call of the outdoors before we become hothouse plants and have to say, "I can't take it."

The grandest life in the world is in the out of doors—nature in the rough. Elemental life— where storms play symphonies that interweave themes from the gurgling brooks and rushing creeks, varied by staccato sleet and rain increased into the demonic splendor of the wind; returning to the reposeful triumph as the sun bursts through the clouds. Storm or sunshine, it's God's weather and all weather is good.

When you build a roof over Your Cabin in the Woods for warmth and security, and stay within that cabin, you shut out the sky. Instead, think of your living room as the out of doors.

My friend John A. Stiles wrote, "There is no such thing as bad weather, only improper clothing. Who cares whether it is raining or not, as long as he is prepared for it? Have you ever asked yourself if you like rain? I love to stride along with the rain beating in my face. How wonderful to come home with your feet going squash, squash in your boots—then to take a hot bath, a rub down, and sit before the fire reading a book, your body all aglow with the exercise, the bath, and the increased circulation."

How grand to have a friend to share this enthusiasm. I, too, like to hike through a storm, tucked into a long raincoat. Try spending half an hour sitting on a log watching the animal life before or after a storm. Stormy weather will bring you closer together. Squirrel and I seem to be buddies, drawn closer through delight, perhaps fear, of the storm. We like the fierce wild weather.

But let's get back to weather signs. "It's going to rain." How do we know? First, a shift of the wind. The lowering cloud ceiling announced by the swallows circling low. Gray nimbus clouds gather. Thunderheads pile up on the horizon. The robins' rain song. The small animals scurry for shelter. The herd of cattle huddled together. You, with eyes to see and wit to interpret, need no barometer to forecast a storm. There are signs, too, for the weather wise that guide spring planting, that warn of a long hard winter. "Deep snow this year," says the farmer. "Heavy lush foliage and the bees are hiving high. Bees always store honey high in the trees when snowbanks will be high." So, when you see them making a beeline for the treetops, mark it down there will be heavy snow that winter. "Early winter," says Leo, "rabbits already have their winter fur. Bird migrations are two weeks ahead of last year. Scarcely a berry or nut left to pick up. The creatures are taking no chances."

When you live with the weather, when your livelihood depends upon your awareness, you learn to watch the trembling of the aspens, the turning to the rain of willow and poplar leaves. You pay attention to all the simple signs of changing weather—even the sweat on your water bucket—the sounds—the silences.

Fruit trees bud by the first warmth of spring sun—sometime to an early, false warmth in April. Fruit growers fight to keep their orchards warm for just those few frosty nights. They build smudge fires. They cover their trees with canvas and build fires among the trees. Sometimes they succeed. Sometimes not. Only the oak can be counted on as a weather prophet. In Wisconsin, we planted corn when the oak leaves were the size of squirrels' ears. The oak will not respond to warm weather until it has really come and frosty weather is really gone. Grandma King said, "Never plant cucumbers (in New York State) until June thirteenth. If you do they will be scrawny."

So here you have an introduction to signs and weather signals. An odd mixture of fact and old wives' tales—from rings around the moon to Grandpa's "rhumatiz" or aching corns. It is fun to cultivate the skill to be able to stick your finger dramatically into your mouth, then up above your head and announce with accuracy, "The wind is from the north" as you feel the sharp line of coolness on that side of your finger. We really need this trick when sailing in a small craft.

Funny how we humans think we can command nature. We build cities along the riverbanks, and spend millions of dollars to build levees and dikes to keep out high water. Engineers think they have control but, each year, somewhere, the floods break through, inundating houses, farms, villages, and bridges. Nature shows her power.

This I know: God has an ordered universe. The answers are there to be read. To understand nature is a step toward understanding God. The good green earth belongs to Him. He made the weather signs.

Night Enchantment

SUPPER over and the campfire. Eyes focused upon the flames. We are drawn closer together. Confidences are shared, and friends are in tune. Cooling embers. The moon overhead. Enchantment. A longing. "Time to retire," something within says. Let us pause. Drink deep of the night as we look at the stars—the great beyond. Have you ever really looked searchingly at the stars? Have you really gazed and studied long enough to see not only one million, but two, three, and more millions of twinkling stars—so many, so myriad that finally there is no room in the sky because of them? Do this. Do it long and do it searchingly and you will realize, again and again, that "God is in His heaven."

The Bursting Splendor of Sunrise

AFTER a night's refreshing sleep, there is no sweeter awakener than the morning sunrise of many colors. I love sunrise because it brings a new day, a new opportunity, a new world. Rising early, you will feel refreshed and wide awake. You will discover a peace of mind, relaxed muscles, and, suddenly, an urge to get up and about and do things. You warm yourself twice—first by cutting your firewood, which loosens muscles and stirs the blood. Then, again, in front of your fireplace, campfire, or kitchen stove. The sweet smell of frying bacon, the rich aroma of coffee, and, finally, a "royal" breakfast.

Where is the morning paper full of stock markets, murders, war, births, deaths? Well, sit back, Mr. Cabin-Builder, and enjoy breakfast. Let the world go by. No radio? Tune your ears to the song of the birds and wildlife about you. A cricket may chirp on your hearth. You will find the stillness most restful.

The sun is now over the horizon—many brilliant colors—shifting shadows. It is morning—early morning and a new day. This indeed is a different world.

Woodland
Sounds

There is no place in the whole wide world where one may find sweeter melodies than in the Great Out Doors. God composed the songs for nature and made them vocal. Away, far away from the manmade noises, woodland songs are recorded on the delicate auditory nerve—always rhythmic, satisfying, stirring—if we will only train ourselves to listen.

The clang of streetcars, the blare of automobile horns and sirens, the screech of brakes and tires—city noises have become so natural to us we scarcely realize how they tighten our nerves and dull our ears to the delicate sounds of the outdoors. Indeed, the poignant stillness of one's first day in the woods may be oppressive and lonely. An afternoon is not long enough to establish the closeness, the desire necessary for a mood of receptiveness to what God's Out

shagbark
Hickory

Doors has to give. People in the busy whirl of city life may not retreat long enough in the outdoors to find this great musical secret—indeed, phenomenon. It takes almost solitude for a few days—or awayness with a companion with whom you are in tune. Tune not only your ear, but also yourself, to the quiet. Turn the dials of your human radio down, down to the wavelength of the wind's whisper. It takes patience, relaxation, time, but the inspiration, the refreshment, is worth it—and more! A new song world is yours for the taking. Zephyrs flowing through the trees, causing idle leaves to laughingly brush one another. Breezes and winds sigh or roar. It is a singing world we live in—from the trickling stream, the gurgling water as it falls over rocks, to mating songs of birdland, and the wailing, warning, and wooing calls of wild creatures. Even the grander sounds of the rhythmic pattern of pounding ocean waves and driving storms have music.

Red Oak

white Oak

Wind, in its many moods, is always musical. The varied names for the wind in its ever-changing tempo are, in themselves, musical. Zephyr, breeze, wind—ring in the ear. Tempest, hurricane, cyclone, typhoon—dangerous in their import—yet sounds that are strong, vibrant, resonant. As a youngster, I used to call across the small valley on our farm, "Heigh-ho!" and "Heigh-ho" came back to me from the rocky

Black
Walnut

cliff in that mystical echo of tempered tones. I called more softly, and the words came back to me no longer raucous, but quiet, reassuring, and soothing. Grownup, I still trek back to the farm (long since in other hands), but the echo is still mine and returns "Heigh-ho" when I call. Ours is a singing world!

I despair today of the brash radio's canned noise. I say "noise," because when sounds are jumbled, discordant, meaningless, they are no longer sounds, but noises. Thomp-thomp—thomp—bass notes; croonings and commercial jingles, squeaks and dronings; screams and shots to add "color" to a bit of lurid mystery and drama. These are noises—not music.

Music had its beginning in the sounds of Nature's Great Out Doors—whispering winds, laughing springs, babbling brooks, and rustling leaves. The deep notes of the croaking bullfrog, the hum of the bee, the high-pitched call of the goldfinch on the wing—the rumble and crash of thunder, the scream and roar of the windstorm. Wagner, Grieg, Tchaikovsky, Beethoven, and the other immortals, through their magnificent symphonic music, have portrayed woodland sounds for man.

But we need not always go to manmade concerts for our inspiration. Sit on a tree stump and relax, without "fuss or feather," or the price of a front-row seat. Tune your ear to the song of

White
Ash

the brook. Hark to the meadowlark as she welcomes spring from the fields still brown and dull. Listen to the catbird's mimicry, the cardinal's mellow whistle, the plaintive mourning dove and hermit thrush as they greet the twilight. Move to the edge of your lily pond, to the cheery assurance of the peepers. Drink deep the vibrant melodies of an awakening world. Sit on your cabin veranda and enjoy the majestic sounds of the Storm King, the gusts of wind singing as they rush through the trees. Note the homey sounds a storm brings to life—the old hanging saw on the woodshed hums, the taut clothesline whines, a loose shingle or an overhanging branch beats rhythmically.

As a boy, I was once told of the "Master Violin Builder" who created a giant violin by stretching wires across a great valley and pulling them taut. Nary a sound from them until the gentle breeze increased to gale velocity. As harder and harder it blew, there came from the strings a heavenly harmony of sound and song, mild and deep tones mingled with those on high, until heaven sang forth a great symphony and those who heard it were lifted and inspired.

So tune your ear to the simple and beautiful music of woodland sounds. God composed these songs to lift our hearts—if we will but listen.

When the Snow Is Deep

IT is wintertime. The snow is deep. Cold frosty night settles. Snow begins to drift. Then from earth and heaven, a billowing storm of crystal flakes bites your face. Toes tingle and legs twinge with the in-and-out pull against the drifts. Time for snowshoes and skis. Cover your ears. Pull up your collar. Tuck your chin into your muffler and keep going. A good steady gait will stir the blood and warm you as you carry your pack on your back.

Just where are we going on this bleak, frosty, stormy night? We have left the city far behind. The car is parked on top of the hill in the barn of a neighborly farmer. We (my wife and I) hear a call from the wild as we trudge to our cabin. Is it a dog, a coyote, a wolf? The dark shadow of our cabin looms through the storm—black, cold, forbidding. The trick latch quickly opens the door. Tinder and kindling prepared on the last trip lie ready for the match. Shadows yield to the glowing, sparkling fires in stove and fireplace. Cold changes to warmth and we peel off our snowy outer garments. Within the hour, our cabin will be

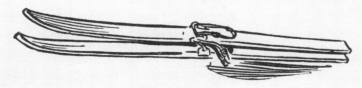

ready to reward our four expected guests with its warm radiance, fragrant with steaming coffee.

They come. Each laden with packsacks of duffel, woolens, food, and fixings for the weekend. (No going back to the grocery store for added supplies.) Such an adventure calls for careful planning. On snowshoes or skis, they trudge breathlessly up the last slope. I go out to meet them as I hear their merry shouts and laughter, and help pull the toboggan, now laden with duffel. Tomorrow it will be ready to give fun and excitement. Packs are lowered onto the piles of cordwood sheltered on the porch. We stomp our feet and pant our greetings—breathing deep. The kitchen broom comes into play as we sweep each other free of clinging snow. Finally, all are inside, toasting "fore and aft" before the blazing warmth. We need to dry out a bit.

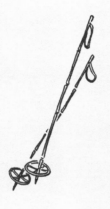

Do you, now, my reader, feel "goose pimples" and shiver at the thought of sleeping in a cabin on a zero-degree night? Read on a bit. You are missing one of the grandest of winter adventures, a winter weekend in the woods.

If you have sleeping bags or plenty of blankets (four woolen ones are essential), you can nestle in and let the fires go out. If you have less, one of the party must keep watch and rebuild the fires every three hours. Either way,

you will sleep well and dream sweet winter dreams. I keep a half-dozen quilts in the cabin for those guests who may be inexperienced and so are caught a bit short.

Clothes for winter fun should include two pairs of woolen socks, good shoes, an extra pair if you have no overshoes. (I prefer galoshes.) A woolen shirt, a sweatshirt, and, of course, warm underwear. Better get out Grandfather's red woolen undershirt and drawers. No wonder our pioneer fathers "could take it" in the woods— good or bad weather. They were prepared to take nature in their stride. So can we.

The group relaxes. In for the weekend! No cares. No worries. No jangling telephones. The wind howls increasingly, packs the tiniest cracks with insulation of snow that makes the cabin even more secure. Supper is underway. Two kettles of steaming vegetables; fireplace biscuits in the reflector oven. The aroma taxes our patience. But wait no longer. A bowl of savory soup is served to each as we sit about watching the fire's flames and the last act . . . the smoking

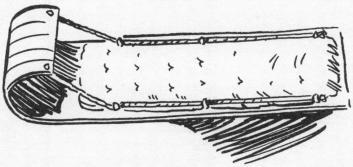

grill. The coals leap into momentary flame as the rich steak grease drips. "Ready with the rare steaks," and the discriminating are fed. A moment more and even the chef admits dinner is a feast for kings.

Cooking over a glowing open fire can be done with a nicety, and to the entertainment of the guests. Sly remarks will be passed. Interesting queries, too, from the cook who knows only the kitchen stove, wood, gas, or electric technique. Fireplace cooking requires a bit of a different skill. Onions and potatoes in their "jackets" are dropped deep into the fireplace and covered with four inches of coals. Leave them for an hour. Dig them out, brush off the ash. You never tasted the like.

The fire dies down a bit. The candles on the table flicker softly. Deep contented sighs and easy conversation rise. Someone draws the last delicious drops from the copper coffee kettle. The movement breaks the spell and the group is in action once again. All the lamps are lighted. The kitchen crew cleans up, for we've found half the fun comes from sharing all of the living in the Cabin in the Woods. The smoldering logs are set ablaze with a small piece or two of wood. Wood for the night, kindling for the morning are brought in. Beds made snug and tight to climb into. Food is prepared against spoiling or freezing. The icebox will keep the cold out in winter if the temperature is zero. An added hot brick will keep it warm. We are ready for the evening fun.

Out comes the box of games. Bridge? Anagrams for the wordsters? Jigsaws? Monopoly? Sometimes we just yarn, cracking hickory and walnuts gathered in the fall. Sometimes we vie at toasting marshmallows or try our skill at candle dipping. Whatever the beginning of a winter evening, the end is always the same— the magic of the quiet—of the leaping flames— inspiring security, and our deeper thoughts well up in that last half-hour before going to bed. The chill of night is held back by the gleam of fire on the hearth. The curling flames and smoke are in control. When February winds are most persistent at the windows, when drifting snow gathers at the corner of each pane, our fireplace is a glowing, yes, a living symbol of the warmth and security of home and family and friends. It warms the feet, hands, and body, but it also warms the heart. The slow, steady glow of the backlog, the spit and sparkle of the deep lingering coals stir warm companionship, invite imagination, philosophies, close confidence.

Friendliness

WHAT is sweeter in life than friendliness? If there is any place in the world that will produce friendliness and kindliness, it is the out of doors. Did you ever have that rich experience of sleeping in a tent with a friend who got up quietly in the morning without disturbing you, rebuilt the campfire of the night before, and started the day's program? After reheating the double boiler of porridge that had been steaming all night, instead of saying to you, "Get up, old man, don't expect me to do all the work," he waits until the aroma of cooking bacon and coffee waft their way toward you. Suddenly you arouse, stretch your arms, and say, "Why I have only slept ten minutes." You have really slept like a child and here your friend has added to your happiness in getting the breakfast. So down to the creek to make your toilet; back refreshed and then to do justice to an unrationed appetite. Describe and do it justice? Who can? You must live through it.

The chipmunk on the nearby stump where you placed food cautiously steals up, blinks one of his little bright eyes at you, and seems to say,

"I like your friendliness." Birds come down to your feeding station—perhaps a bit cautious at first, but they come. Having been served a "royal" breakfast, you now will want to take your share of the load by cleaning up camp. If on a hike your partner develops a sore toe or blister, you say with nonchalance, "Give me your pack. I'll carry it." That's friendliness.

The trail in the woods is friendly. One does not stalk with heavy feet through the woods, but with the lithe tread so as not to disturb the wildlife. Go through the woods lightly and with music in your heart. As you trail through the woods, you will be amazed to find nature full of "signs, signals, and symbols." These, too, are friendly signs if you can read them. True you will find no highway marked "Route 20," but every trail is marked equally effective by Mother Nature. There are signs that tell you a spring is near, where to find food, of approaching storms. We need only to learn them, to find that nature is friendly and eager to tell us through her method of signs and symbols how to enjoy wildlife. She guards her secrets from those who treat them lightly, but gives of them willingly to those who study her ways.

Approval

NOW we come to the most important part of our discussion—the need for a right attitude toward life; a balanced understanding of what brings security to us. Out of that friendliness built through experience one with another comes the very foundation of the good life. No four people could go up into the wilds of Canada and live for a week or more together and have one of the four a "drone." Each must carry his share of the load. National wealth comes out of honest hard labor and effort of the individual "to earn a little and to spend a little less." Somehow, in our cities there creeps into our communal life poachers, parasites, people who live off other people. They contribute little to the world, but, in the Great Out Doors, in this whole field of friendliness, comes this conception of building a democracy. The desire of one to do a little more than his share to add to the happiness of the group.

I have seen over and over when a group of six or eight camp together, one will be selfish, self-centered, stingy, greedy. After a period of a week or two in the woods with friends, he comes back a changed person. It may mean a bloody nose. The treatment may be a bit severe from his peers, but he will finally carry his share of the load if he has the fortitude to "take it" and stand by. Then, some day, one of the boys will make up his bed and he will come in and say, "Who has been monkeying with my bed?" The next lad will say, "Well, you carried in wood today and I sort of thought I would help you out." Something tremendous is happening to this selfish lad. It will take a day or two before he will do a kindness in return, but, before the camp is over, he will give a good account of himself. When he returns home, he may say to his father, "Do you mind if I cut the lawn today?" No, he has just learned to carry his share of the load.

If you were to say to me, "You can broil the best steaks in the world," I'd just swell with pride and love it, and I'd try harder to justify that approval you have given me. You know what I mean by the glow that comes to you when someone slaps you on the back and says, "You did the job well. You conducted an inspiring campfire." Recognition comes from our friends who not only approve of us, but, in the approving, also indicate they think well of us. In slang we hear, "He is a good egg. He is the kind who can take it on the chin. A regular fellow."

To be in tune with the outdoors you must have a song in your heart and the song gives its own approval. Perhaps the most material proof you are a "regular fellow" comes from the little chipmunk on the stump who no longer pays any attention to you—has taken you in as a part of the woods. And the squirrel overhead no longer scolds, but accepts you. The birds that come to your feeding stations and pay no attention; when your friends like to be with you, not because of your money, not because of your influence, or any possible superior advantage or abilities, but just because you are you—a balanced individual—a regular fellow.

When you merit all these the world will salute you as a master camper, a partner, a friend. You have learned the art of living happily together with folks, with nature, with wildlife in the woods. Most of all, you have learned to live comfortably with yourself.

The Latchstring Is Out

AND now we must part. As I said in the first chapter, I pictured you sitting on a log while I nestled against a notch in a big tree, talking over the project of building a Cabin in the Woods. So I say farewell with a real twinge of regret.

Conrad E. Meinecke

About the Author

BORN of sturdy pioneer parents in a northern Wisconsin log cabin in 1883, Conrad Meinecke's youth was spent ruggedly outdoors. He worked on a farm with his family, roamed the woods with Native Americans, hiked across the prairies, climbed the Rockies, fished in Canada, and traveled in Europe, Asia Minor, and North Africa. During that time he learned how to make himself and his companions comfortable under all kinds of conditions. These experiences also taught him to understand and love mankind. He lived by the motto "We all walk this road together, none goes his way alone. All that we give into the lives of others . . . comes back to our own."

This was reflected in Meinecke's career as a social worker, including time as the director of men and boy's work for the Westminster House Social Settlement in Buffalo. He then ran the boys home for the Buffalo Children's Aid Society. From 1923 to 1948, he was the chief executive of the Buffalo NY Boy Scout Council, during which time he developed a number of camps, including a 1,200-acre complex in Schoellkopf, New York.

As a hobby, Meinecke was a cabin and wood craft builder. He constructed scores of cabins scattered throughout the United States and Canada. He received many requests to put all of his accumulated wisdom on the subject of cabin building into book form.

In 1944, Meinecke wrote his first book, titled *Your Cabin in the Woods*, which was filled with cabin lore and his own simple philosophy of living. He printed the first edition on a small press in his home and bound it in cloth laced together with cord. In 1945 the book was published by Foster & Stewart Publishing. In 1947, he wrote his second book, titled *Cabin Craft and Outdoor Living*, also published by Foster & Stewart.

Wishing to maintain closer contact with his readers, he formed the Darnock Cabin Craft Guild for the interchange of ideas between cabin builders. Membership was free and thousands of members were scattered all over the world.

Meinecke died in March 1971 in his log cabin in Springville, New York.

Index

Page numbers in italics refer to illustrations

A

Animals, 248–250, 262–265
  animal tracks
    cottontail rabbit, 10, 12
    raccoon, 11
    red fox, 9
    skunk, 10, 12
    squirrel, 11
    white tailed deer, 9
  birds, 175–176
Architecture
  amateur architect, 51–*58*
  architectural planning, *54*, 55–56
  blueprints, 20
  building rules, 73–74
  model building, 57–58
Axes, 66–68

B

Blueprints
  cabins, *31, 38, 41, 43, 44, 45, 46, 47,*
    48, 49, 50
  creation of, 20

fireplaces, *101, 102, 103, 109*
foundation, *84*
roof, *84, 142*
tents, *33*

C

Cabins
  construction of
    log binding, 79–85
      Maine-woods method, *82,*
        82–85, 84
    log chinking, 89–91, *90*
    log types, 77–79
    V-studs, 82–85, 84
  cost of, 76–77
  family cabin, 27–34
    floor plan, 30
    legend, 29
  four-room cabin, 42–50, *43*
    AA
      blueprint, 45
    Chief's Lodge
      floor plan, 44
    floor plan, 43

Long House
    blueprint, *48*
    floor plan, *49*
Shingle Shakes
    blueprint, *46*
    floor plan, *47*
The Squatter
    blueprint, *50*
frame house, 141–143
    novel log effect, 143, *143*
guest cabin, 27–34
    floor plan, *31*
location of, 20
note-taking, 18, 20
one-room cabin, 38–39
    blueprint, *38*
planning for the future, 19–24
planning overview, 11–12, 19–20, 74
sizing of accommodations, 26–36
storm porch, 40, *41*
two-room cabin, 40–42
    blueprint, *41*
Camping, 191–204, 238–247,
    251–252
    cooking on a spit jack, 216–218, *217,*
        233–235, *234*
    cooking with a reflector oven, *231,*
        231–233
    family camp grounds
        floor plan, *30–31*
        legend, *29*
Cooking, 110, *111,* 206–236, *224,*
    226, 231, 234. See also recipes
    picnic, 237

Doors, 53, 87, 90
    latches, hinges and shutter catches,
        124, 124–125, *125*
    storm doors, 137
    trick door with secret lock, *138,* 139

Fireplaces, 12, 27, 53, 87, 91–112,
    92, 95, 125, 206–213
    and ashes, 93–95, 110–112
    chimney, 106–107, 206–209
    construction of, 99–110, *109*
        tools and materials, 105
    cooking grate, *111*
    fire place screen, *111*
    fire place tools, *111*
    foundation, 106–107
    outdoors, 206–211, 212–213, *224*
    pot hooks, 110
    Raised Hearth fireplace
        cross section, *102*
        plan and detail, *101, 109*
    Small Brick fireplace
        plan and detail, *103*
    W. I. andirons
        detail, *105*
    W. I. arm for pots, 107
    and wood for burning, 96–98
Floors, 90, 125–126, 144–145
Foot scrapers, *127*
Foundation, 51–52, 73, *84, 85,* 87
    fireplace and chimney, 106–108
Furniture, 55, 88, 131–137
    bedding, 88, 137
    dining, *131,* 131–134, *132, 133, 134*
    seating, 88, *135,* 135–136, *136*

G

Great out doors, 11, 15–17, 238–276
animals, 248–250, 262–265
  birds, 175–176
  camping, 191–204
  cooking, 206–236, *224, 226, 231, 234*
  picnics, 236
  springs, 185–188
  trails, 182–184
Grindstone, 64–65

H

Houses
  frame house, 141–143

I

Insulation
  chinking, 89–91, *90*
Interior design, 88, 123–139
  coat hangers, 139
  floors, 90, 125–126, 144–145
  furniture, 55, 88, 131–137
    bedding, 88, 137
    dining, *131,* 131–134, *132, 133, 134*
    seating, 88, *135,* 135–136, *136*
  lighting, *122,* 125, *128,* 128–130
    lanterns, *129,* 129–130, *130*
  rugs, 126

K

Kitchen, 40
  cooking outside, 206–236, *224, 226, 231, 234*
  ice box cooler, 140
  picnics, 236
Knives, 69–71

L

Land
  cost of, 75–76
  drainage and grading, 87–88
Landscaping, 150–168
  gateways, guardrails and fences, 177–181
    Alamo, 179
    Chinook, 178
    Garrison, 178
    Pioneer, 178
    Swanee, 181
    Western, 181
    Yankee, 181
  steppingstones, *145,* 145–146
  trails, 182–184
Lighting, *122,* 125, *128,* 128–130
  lanterns, *129,* 129–130, *130*
Living simply, 11–12, 21–22, 75, 272–276
Logs
  binding, 79–85
    Maine-woods method, 82, 82–85, 84
  chinking, 89–91, *90*
  notching, 81, *81*
  novel log effect, 143, *143*
  types for construction, 77–79
  types for furniture, 123–124

N

Nails, 71–73
Nature, 11, 15–17, 20, 238–276
   camping, 191–204
   cooking, 206–236, *224, 226, 231, 234*
   maple sugaring, 169–174
   picnic, 236
   springs, 185–188
   trails, 182–184

P

Painting and staining, 88–89
Plants
   chicory, 188
   curled dock, 187
   Indian cucumber, 185
   wild mint, 186
Plumbing, 115–118
   septic system, 117
   toilet, 40–41, *41,* 116–118
   water system and supply, *114,* 115

R

Recipes
   baked beans, 221, *221*
   cheese and crackers, 222–223
   chili, 220–221
   corn pone, 232–233
   dinner on a spit jack, 233–235, *234*
   fireplace cinnamon toast, 223
   hamburgers, 216
   hot dog, bacon and melted cheese
      dream, 221–222
   Hunter's stew, 216–218, *217*
   New England boiled dinner, 219
   perpetual pancakes, 232
   potatoes, 218
   Red Flannel hash, 219–220
   reflector oven biscuits, *231,* 231–232
   rolled roast of beef, 223–225, *224*
   Shore dinner lobster pot, *226,*
      226–231
   steak, 214–216
Roof, 39, 41, 55–56, 57, 79–80, *84,*
   102
   roof plates at corners, 141, *142*
   tent roof, 32–34, *33*

T

Tents, 32–34
   guest tent, *32*
      blueprint, 33
      floor plan, 34
Tools, 61–90
   axes, 66–68
   care of, 63–65
   grindstone, 64–65
   knives, 69–71
   nails, 71–73
   toolbox, 61–62
      contents of, 63–64
   tool shed, *60,* 63

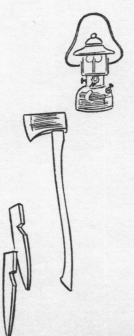

Trees
   Black Walnut, 264
   Red Oak, 263
   Shagbark Hickory, 262
   White Ash, 263
   White Oak, 263

U

U. S. Department of Agriculture
   Farmers' Bulletin No. 1649, 104

V

Ventilation, 86–87, 126

W

Waste disposal, 118–120
   incinerators, 118–119
Windows, 35–36, 53, 85–87, 90
   sky lights, 140
   sliding window, *86*
Winter, 267–271
Wood stove, 102, 109, 126–127,
   209-211